Life AFTER HER!

A Story in Honor of *Teenie*

KEVIN BAILEY

Copyright © 2022 Kevin Bailey

All rights reserved. No part of this document may be reproduced or transmitted in any form or by any means, electronic, mechanical, photocopying, recording, or otherwise, without prior written permission of the author.

LIFE AFTER HER
A Story In Honor of Teenie

Kevin Bailey
Kevin.Bailey1946@gmail.com

ISBN 978-1-943342-19-8

Printed in the USA.
All rights reserved

Published by: Destined To Publish | Flossmoor, Illinois
www.DestinedToPublish.com

PREFACE

This autobiography is and will be a source of healing for me, as well as telling my story from my perspective after the passing of my mother: the one and only Evelyn Bailey, a.k.a. Teenie! This book is not intended to offend, be divisive, adversely affect or negatively impact anyone in my life or otherwise connected to me, but to symbolize a period of growth, elasticity and stretching, grief and epiphanies that occurred after March 19, 2000, at 6 p.m. This date and time, all the way down to the aura of the whole room and the sadness on everyone's faces, this was the most pivotal moment in my life I would experience as a 28 year-old man. Hopefully, this book provides a window into the Christian perspective of an African-American urban family as it relates to family dynamics in the 1970s, 1980s, 1990s and beyond. Moreover, it highlights the positive effects of having a loving and strong relationship between mother and son, an unbreakable bond, as well as how I dealt with the grief of her death and her afflictions of Lupus and Diabetes.

Moreover, I value the relationships and experiences I have developed over the years and in the time period described in this book, whether positive or negative, because it's those relationships and situations that have developed me into the person I am today and allowed me to grow into my purpose and mission in life for my future.

Believe it or not, I struggle with fear! Fear of being a disappointment or burden to my family, of not living up to the standard of who I was raised to be and, for that matter, who I should be as a father, brother, husband and friend. I grapple with where I am in life and where I need to be for my family. After all, at the end of the day, we do what we do for our families, right? We are who we are even when no one is looking, watching or seeing what you're doing. No matter where you go in life, you're still taking that person you are or have become with you, whatever your destination ultimately evolves into.

A quote from my mother: "Finish what you start, and don't start nothing you can't finish!" The time is now! It's time to finish the fervent work she put in me to finish. Mom, you asked me not to forget about you, but to remember you. Mom, no, I've never forgotten about you and never will! Our bond is an eternal chain, like the umbilical cord you used to nurture and develop me when I was an infant inside your womb.

This book will delve into the bond of mother and son. You see, I'm learning that mothers train their daughters but raise their sons. Why is that? Parenting is universal, right? But it has been said, "The biological bond between a mother and her son is one of the strongest bonds ever established in life." This saying is very true, in multiple respects.

Prepare yourself for this journey of words… You will laugh (hopefully not at me but with me!), you will cry and perhaps even get angry too. But understand that these are the thoughts, feelings, experiences and challenges I have dealt with or have overcome after my mother's death. I am sharing with the intention that you will grow too, learn something and develop into your calling, gift and purpose in life!

FOREWORD

By Tracy Allen

I'm Tracy Allen. Evelyn "Teenie" Thomas Bailey was my godmother, whom I affectionately referred to as "Aunt Tina," and she was "Big Sis" to my mother, Wendy Allen. She was acquainted with both of my parents and their families from very early years. One of her younger brothers (Ernest), my dad (John), and my Uncle Herbert (my mom's family) were all really good friends who hung out frequently. So this extended family of love got started by the Baileys adopting the Allen's, so to speak.

Kevin Lee Bailey, the center son and author of *Life, After Her*, became my ally in shenanigans. We're six months and six days apart (March 23, 1972 / September 29, 1972). I'm the oldest always and forever, no computation needed, but he still (in real time, right now), refuses to comply.... Big Sis/Lil Bro. He honored his

Aunt Wendy and me with the assignment of writing this piece for the book, and we accepted without hesitation. I struggled painfully, not because I lacked in thoughts or memories of her, but because it was yet another devastating reminder that she's not physically present with us.

> Wendy Allen wrote:
>
> Her second son, my nephew, is chronicling in this book through his eyes the vital role "Big Sis" portrayed in so many lives as a wife, mother, grandmother, daughter, sister, aunt, godmother, friend, etc., all while remaining a true Woman of God (First Lady). She could mingle with the most sanctified and the biggest sinners, not once changing who she was or what she represented… RESPECT, LOYALTY, DIGNITY. She always gave it all and required nothing less from anyone, and if you tried it, she would put you right back in your place with a Godlike quickness that any walk of life understood.

Elegant. Tenacious. Warrioress. Proverbs 31. This is genuinely who my godmother "Aunt Tina" was and still is for me. These words came to me effortlessly as descriptors of the woman I knew and loved. As I double-checked that the meanings were accurate to what I wanted to express, the scripture Proverbs 31 came up in my search for a strong woman of God. Feel free to look up the definitions of these words if you're unfamiliar with them. Many lifetimes can pass, but it will never erase her imprint in the thoughts, memories, or hearts of us who were blessed to experience all the love, wisdom, time, and guidance Evelyn "Teenie" Thomas Bailey shared intentionally and unselfishly.

Eternal Love,

Wendy and Tracy Allen

TABLE OF CONTENTS

Section I: Family Dynamic 1
- Church upbringing
- Family Traveling to Muskogee, OK
- Learning what a friend is vs. associate
- Gaining Independence and confidence
- Learning Humility
- The women she was… "do good"

Section II: Trying of our Faith. 39
- Afflictions
- Her life pivot
- Graduation of a young lion
- Heartfelt separation – "do good"

Section III: All things work together 47
- Grooming of a Bailey man
- Reversing the curse in our lineage
- Her educational encouragement
- Symbolism of three
- Lions do not swim
- Overcoming adversity – "do good"

Section IV: Culmination of it all 58
- The plan for growth
- Earning my degree
- Images of a lion pride
- How I grieved your loss
- Your legacy
- Last request to a son

Final: This is it… 100
- Poem of Mrs. Bailey
- My final letter to mom – "do good"
- Letters of a sister - tribute

SECTION I
Family Dynamic

My earliest memory of being a Bailey was around 1975. I was born in 1972; we lived in an apartment complex on Parallel Parkway in Kansas City, KS, called Victory Hills. I'm not sure where the name came from, but nevertheless, it was home. During that time, it was my father, mother and only brother: – Charles O. Bailey, Sr., Evelyn (Thomas) Bailey (a.k.a. Teenie) and Charles O. Bailey, Jr. (a.k.a. Chuck) – plus me, Kevin Lee Bailey. The Lee was after my uncle, Lee Thomas, a very respected figure in the Kansas City Police Department. He and his partner Mr. Hooks were two of the first African-American patrol officers in the Kansas City, KS, area. Uncle Lee attended Pittsburg State

University and was a Kappa man. Because I was only about three years of age at the time, please understand that while my memory goes back to that point, I am limited to only a few instances.

During that era, men played an important role in my life, shaping me and molding me to be mentally, physically and spiritually strong. See, back in my era of growing up, it was intentional to pour into young men the things necessary to deal with what life might throw at them in their future. Keep in mind, those lessons taught were predicated on the previous generation's values and the ethics of the values taught to those who are teaching you.

Our home was a traditional patriarch and matriarch-structured home. My father was raised Pentecostal, Church of God in Christ (COGIC) – yes, the rowdy and charismatic bunch of churchgoers. We had the Holy Ghost "and that with fire," as the old saint often said! My mother was a member at Tabernacle Baptist Church in Kansas City, KS, the only pink church building I think I have ever seen in my life. So, based on the structure of our home, we attended a Pentecostal church, Lakeside Church of God in Christ. King S. Davis was our pastor. We were from that rowdy bunch, believing in the laying on of hands, gift of tongues and shouting (spiritual dancing and worship only expressed in utterances to the Most High)! You know, speaking in tongues, shouting, hands on folks in prayer, with the hopes of manifesting life-changing miracles and blessings.

We believed in having church for hours in a day. Our weekly church schedule was Tuesday night prayer and choir rehearsal, Thursday night prayer and Bible study, Sunday School starting at 9:45 a.m., then morning worship at 11 a.m. and services going until around 2 p.m. or 2:30 p.m., again depending on the flow of the Spirit during service or how long testimony service lasted. Now, keep in mind, once a month we had district meeting, where six to eight different churches (usually in the same city) would gather together for an afternoon church service from 3:30 p.m. to around 5:30 or 6 p.m. – again, depending on the flow of the Spirit. So, once a month, on Sunday, we would basically be in church all day, because after district meeting, we'd have YPWW (Young People Willing Workers) back at our church. Remember, we were just kids, in school, trying to be normal and do our homework. You would have to be sick or at least act like it to avoid being at church all the time. Sometimes if you were sick, they'd take you anyway and just pray for you there, so it didn't always work!

In those days, it was frowned on to go to church for an hour or less. That meant you didn't spend enough time with God, giving back to Him a portion of what He's given you! After all, Sunday is the Sabbath day – keep it holy! No work, just praising Him and lifting Him up! Sunday was designed for God and family only.

Now, we did have some fun at Lakeside Church. I remember when our Young People Willing Worker, Y.P.W.W., group went to Six Flags Over Texas, near Dallas. The Harden's were a family we attended church with at Lakeside Church. They were beloved; they were the first African American family that owned a functional farm. We stayed with Brother and Sister Harden's relatives; it was in a townhome, so there were teenage bodies lying everywhere, but we were all together, so it really didn't matter. That was family! From those trips, we traveled more as the Bailey family. We went to Washington D.C., Minnesota (several times), Muskogee, Oklahoma (almost annually), and

Denver, Colorado (including the summit of Pikes Peak). Short story: When we were coming down from Pikes Peak, Chuck's asthma kicked in due to the higher-than-normal elevation, and Durail Allen Bailey (Allen, my youngest brother) was sick too – he threw up all over the back seat of the car. Boy, those were the days… traveling as a family! In fact, that's where Chuck and I learned to drive on the highway. Our trips to Muskogee were what we looked forward to the most.

My Aunt Coretta was the one of the most loving ladies I ever knew as a kid. She would wake up around 5:30 a.m., sit on the front porch with my parents, talk and share good times together. Then around 6 a.m., she and my mother would set up the table in the dining room and make pancakes, biscuits, sausage and bacon for breakfast. Those two ladies understood taking care of their families, children, jobs and husbands. I know, because I witnessed it! In fact, they both worked in hospitals; Aunt Coretta was a Registered nurse (RN) and my mother was a Licensed Practical Nurse (LPN).

We enjoyed hanging out with our cousins Pierre, Valenta and Lynn. Lynn and I were close in age; she was two or three years older than me. But she always had girlfriends, and any girlfriend of the family was a girlfriend for me too! Yep, I learned early how to mingle with the girls, get to know them and possibly form a relationship. I got my first smooch from one of my cousin's friends up the street. After that trip, I looked forward to going back just to see her again, but she moved. My big cousin Pierre would also walk us all through the neighborhood on our bikes or mini-motor bikes (lawnmower engines). We went over Uncle D's (Deloyd Reed, Aunt Coretta's husband) parents' house (Momma and Poppa Reed's) and to the parks and the lakes.

During those times, we had a camper shell. My dad would put it onto the truck, and we would ride from Kansas City to Muskogee inside the camper shell. My mother would be mad the whole trip until we arrived safely. I think she was afraid the camper shell would fall off with us in it. Back then, the Ford F-150 truck wasn't the most aerodynamic; the wind would get between the back window of the truck and the camper shell and create a turbulent wind noise that made us think we were going to get blown clean off the truck! I guess my mother hated the fact that we were in that situation, but she still tried to trust my father's ability to get us to our destination safely. We stopped frequently to use the bathroom and check the security of the camper shell. I understood then that my dad, as fierce and manly as he was, did not want to feel the heat from my mom.

On other days, when we were not in church, we watched The Cosby Show and boxing matches together while eating soft batch cookies with our dad on the couch. My father was highly motivated to maintain and promote family living, in large part because he was from a broken-home situation. He never had his father under the same roof with him, so he worked fervently to keep us together as a family, as did my mom. It was all intentional, Jeremiah 29:11! In fact, my dad didn't meet his own father until he was around 20 years old, after he was already working a career job and was starting to raise his own family. Speaking of my hero, Dad, he literally broke the curse of fatherlessness without a male role model to show him how to do it – although he did have God on his side! I can only imagine being a responsible man, husband, father, brother, worker and minister all at the same time... He served in all those roles simultaneously without a guide or positive male presence influencing his decision-making. He was a blessing then, and he still plays an integral part in my life to this day.

Being PKs, preacher's kids, we were raised by our father to believe in ourselves, even if others did not. He instilled immeasurable confidence in us to overcome and persevere through obstacles – they will develop, but God will see you through those situations. In fact, James 1:2 tells us that you should be thankful when you're "being tried": *"count it all joy when ye fall into diverse temptations; knowing this, that the trying of your faith worketh patience."* Going through challenges in your life develops and matures your character. The old saints taught us to pray your way out or through a situation and to pray for a lesson from your trials. Why? So that you can be a help to others, because just as you endured it, others will travel the same or similar path you were victorious over. Be a light for them to see their way through it too. Be sincere in all you do, make deliberate your intentions, help, teach and share whenever you can, without looking for something in return. It's in those times when you're not expecting something in return that God can and often will bless you.

I do recall running down the hallways ringing neighbors' doorbells, then hiding to avoid being caught. We limited our mischievous action only to the neighbors we knew. In most cases, they were my mother's female friends; I can't remember all their names. These prank doorbell incidents occurred in Victory Hills Apartments off Parallel in KCK. Not long after that, we moved to 2520 Stewart, just one block north of Parallel Parkway. The exact address was 2520 Stewart, Kansas City, KS 66104, and our phone number was (913) 342-9178. I remember those things because I had to know them in kindergarten; it was required learning.

REFLECTION:

On the west side of our home lived an elderly Polish couple, the Keuchel's. Joseph A. and Amy Josephine Keuchel. Their kids were older than my siblings and me; we met a few of them later in life. Mrs. Keuchel always brought us treats, desserts and candy. The weird thing was that she would knock or ring the doorbell, but then she would just walk right in without being invited, which was weird to me as a young black male. You see, the issue was not that she was not welcome, but that she never allowed us (the home-dwellers) to greet her at the door so that she could be granted access into the home – provided, of course, that everyone in the home was dressed to receive company.

Mrs. Keuchel was an older Polish lady, nice and sweet, yet curious about the black family living next to her. It was then that I noticed Caucasians women can be pushy, imposing and entitled (privileged). Over time, though, I learned that she didn't mean anything by it... it was in her nature. I got the feeling she did not have a lot of experience being around African-American families other than ours. Her curiosity led her conscience; nothing else mattered. You see, respect for our elders was what our parents expected to see in us and for those outside our home to perceive. They instilled this in us, yet forced us to embrace it as well. More or less, Mrs. Keuchel adopted us as her very own, and over time, we learned how to tolerate her behaviors and how to handle her… that is, we just started locking the screen door. (It was a different era in time.)

I need to take this time to personally thank my older brother for extending the life of our mother. She was taking a shower at 2520 Stewart when she fell unconscious inside the shower (with its sliding glass doors) and hit her head on the tile wall. My dad and older brother went to her aid, but my father did not know what to do. My older brother Chuck had just learned CPR, so he gave my mom CPR while the ambulance was en route. Had he not known CPR, we would have been motherless adolescent boys. Thank you, my big brother, for giving our mother CPR – a breath of life! Thank you for being in position in that traumatic moment in our young lives and not only knowing what to do, but being focused enough to handle a pressure-filled moment.

I have driven by our old house many times from a nostalgic perspective; we had a lot of love and memorable moments in that dwelling. For preschool, I attended Wood Haven on State Avenue, near Kensington Park. During those times in the mid- '70s, we walked to school, which was about a 25-minute walk if you used the sidewalks. If you took the shortcuts, it was only 15 minutes, but you had to be ready to run at any given moment. There were dogs loose and roaming the neighborhood, black cats crossing in front of you and just weird folks looking at you – some of them didn't even speak. Generally, in the black community, if someone thought enough of you to speak, the least you could do is speak back out of respect and acknowledgment of another human.

My mother always told me I was an inquisitive and curious child. At the time, I wasn't really sure what that implied, but now

I can see how true it was! At night, as a toddler, I would often wake up to use the restroom to circumvent wetting the bed, which would lead to getting an old-fashioned tanning (whooping or spanking in modern terms). Didn't every kid wet the bed and get a spanking for being lazy and not getting up to use the bathroom once or twice? There was a particular night, I could not sleep, so as I often did, I started downstairs to sleep with my parents or at least let them know I couldn't sleep. When I reached the bottom step and looked through the crack of the door to their room, I noticed my mother sitting vertically up on top of my dad – she was doing some rocking motions and groaning too! Not realizing what was taking place, I watched. Within minutes, my brother noticed I was not in my bed; he too trailed behind me at the bottom of the steps. And nine months later, we had a little brother. Not understanding how this occurred yet, I began asking my mother questions: Where did he come from? Why is he here? And can you send him back? Obviously, none of these questions seemed to matter; he stayed anyway.

It was 1976 when my little brother was born: Durail Allen Bailey, who we affectionately refer to as Dee. I was around four years old, and my older brother was eight. After I realized he wasn't going away anytime soon, I became fond of the little guy, making goofy faces, tickling him or just staring at him. I noticed he got more and more of my attention… that part I didn't appreciate at that time, but over time, I realized and understood that as a sibling and big brother, I was responsible for him – his safety, his understanding/learning and his overall care. At the time, I thought it was cool to have my very own little person to be responsible for. And this is what motivated me to be a beacon of light for him, to be kind of like his hero!

This may seem to be a total contradiction, but as much as I value relationships and true friendship, I can proudly say I lost a friend for the sake of my little brother. While we were living off 27th Street at 2520 Stewart, a blended family of five moved in from Pomona, CA. The father was Iranian, named Mr. Juto, the mother was a nice Caucasian lady (whose name I don't remember) and they had three children, all older than me. Rick was the middle child; he was a junior in high school. I believe the daughter was Susan, and she was expecting a child at the time. Scott was the youngest, about a year and a half older than me; we attended junior high together, rode bikes together and became pretty good friends. At the time, I did not mind dealing with the differences in family dynamics, as long as it gave me some breathing room from my little brother.

One day, while my parents were at church and my brothers and I stayed at home (a rare occasion), I slipped out of the house, leaving my little brother at home with my older brother, to go play with my friends Scott (a ninth-grader) and Lamont (another next-door-neighbor childhood playmate, who lived in the Keuchel' old house after they moved). While we were playing catch in the street, I noticed my little brother approaching. Shucks… he found me! Well, now he wanted to play with everybody. I tried to tell him he was too young and might get hurt, thinking that would persuade him to go back inside the house, right? Wrong. It didn't! Somehow, Dee got the ball. Scott insisted that Dee get out the way, so he started teasing Dee, waving the ball over his head, making Dee jump for the ball because he wanted to participate. As I walked towards the commotion, I saw Scott rub his knuckles across my brother's head, which was violation #1 – my mother taught us to defend ourselves, and not to start fights but to finish them! Dee was getting angry, so he kicked towards Scott's shin, but he didn't connect. Scott then actually kicked Dee (violation #2), and by that time, I was approaching with fists swinging. The next thing I remember is all the neighbors watching and cheering… fight, fight, fight! It was surreal! I remember boxing in the middle of the street, then in Scott's yard and back to the street. Mr. Juto, Scott's stepfather, watched, laughing and smoking a cigarette.

Needless to say, after the fight, Scott and I were no longer friends. We later became playmates again, but it was never the same. It was at that point that the rest of the neighbors knew those "Bailey boys" are a handful. The fight is on – if you mess with one, you might have to fight them all. We *finished* the fight that day, just like Momma told us to do! I lost a friend, but I strengthened the bond with my little brother, which has solidified our brotherhood for life! I love that dude! Guess I'll always look out for him for life. But isn't that what family does? Look out for the home front and never let outsiders cause division among the family, right? Well, that's how we were raised in the Bailey household. Not as thugs, but as productive family-oriented gentlemen who would go to gentlemen lengths – or fists, when necessary – to protect the family and household!

As far as school, I went to Wood Haven on State Ave., across from Kensington Park, which was an integrated school. That was where I learned that I was not white, but black. My mother told me that one day, I came home from school and asked her, "Am

I white?" Why did I ask that question – because I was curious, recall? Plus, my environment reflected that, the early onset of colorism, so I asked the question in all sincerity just so I could know for myself.

After Wood Haven, I started going to Chelsea Elementary School. Chuck and I walked to school together. I was in kindergarten with Miss Hawkins, and he was in fifth grade with Miss Etter. Because I would have a half-day of school, my dad would pick me up most of the time. However, Miss Etter allowed me to sit in her class for the remainder of the day on occasion so I could walk home with my brother. One day, the walk home was horribly disrupted! I'm not sure why, but my brother and I got jumped on. (Why were we always in fights? That's a rhetorical question.) I remember walking across the street at the crosswalk on Parallel, and an older kid stuck me with a stickpin. When we got to the other side, I hit him square in the month. The fight was on after that. The odds were 2:4 or 5. Bad odds, but we didn't back down! We didn't win either. I just remember the Turner kids (another black family, our neighbors across the street) just standing there watching, which made me view them differently after that – they didn't even help. Not sure why, but that made me feel some kind of way towards that family and the kids in that house for the rest of our childhood in that neighborhood. They weren't anything like Roy Mimbs, my other big brother in the hood. Because we were a community, we treated one another like family. Plus, Mrs. Mims was the 70's version of community early start. Thus I knew Roy like a brother. Roy was the youngest male in a family of 8.

Years later, at Chelsea, I was in the fifth grade and Dee was in the first grade. Even then, he was the biggest kid in his class, but everybody knew he was my little brother. We walked to school with Denise (Dee-Dee) from across the street. That was always fun because we played along the way. It wasn't so bad having my little brother tagging along then. As you told me then, Mom, I was responsible for him, and Chuck reinforced it: "He's your responsibility, take care of him!" I guess that's somewhat innate for us to care about one another so deeply. As our parents, thanks for not letting us physically fight as youngsters. Later in life, we still don't fight; we may have disagreements but never fistfights. Family division is horrible, and I've always despised it, especially as a kid.

Middle school started at Northwest Jr. (NWMS) in sixth grade; I played the trumpet in band and drums for the girls' drill team. At that time, we had to report to T.A. (teacher assistance – a teacher who was your homeroom teacher, advisor and mentor) each morning before classes commenced. Ours was Mrs. Tombing, who was the choir teacher; she had attended an HBCU, and she was easy on the eyes. My band teacher was Mr. Derrick Hibler, who had also attended an HBCU; my P.E. teacher was Ms. Jones. The other P.E. teacher was Mr. Stamps. Our vice principal was a fair and cool kind of guy named Mr. Wilson. In fact, he owned a liquor store off Parallel, not too far from NWMS.

The major male influence in my life back then was our principal, Mr. Carl Bruce, a clean-cut gentleman who always wore a suit, dress socks, dress shoes and tie and had a special confidence, smile and a distinguished look. He did not play! I later discovered he was a Kappa Man – shout out to the good Nupe who influenced me from way back (God rest his soul). Yet it was like all of us students were his kids. He cared about us! And he knew how to show us. I presume he was a father to the fatherless, a mentor and a positive African-American male role model to the school and community too. Although he would discipline you, he would also attend, show up and cheer for all athletic teams within the school. Everyone admired him! So, as you can see, I had a strong cultural model structured around me as a young man. I was nurtured to be successful and have tenacity, carry myself with pride and fear no one, but be respectful and polite. After all, that's the least I could do as a youngster, until they showed me otherwise.

Academically, at NWMS, I was in reading and math lab. They would put us at a desk with three sides walled off so you could not be distracted or distract others. Each lab class, they would have us work on fundamental concepts of math or reading. After you successfully completed a full lesson, then and only then would you be able to move on to the next lesson in that subject. Even though the intent was for skills building, I hated those labs! There was a sense of being mentally inferior or not up to par with your peers; I guess that was what fueled and motivated me both directly and indirectly. But, again, I was determined to be successful so I could get the heck out of those classes.

While living at 2520 Stewart, we met Felicia, our sister. She had a different mom than we did, but I never cared… she was my sister. I would affectionately call her "my Fefe." Man, I was so excited to have a sister! I remember meeting Mark, my sister's husband; she brought him by our house to meet all of us, her family. When Felicia had Brandon and Jasmine, I felt so big, it's safe to say I swelled with pride! I felt like as an uncle, I was in position to make a positive impact on their lives in some small way. We built a great relationship and bond. Often, in college, I'd come home for the weekend and would willingly give up spending time with my girlfriend (Lorie) to spend time with them, even though they were young. We'd go to either McDonald's playground or the park, or sometimes I'd just hang out at my sister's house with them. She allowed me to be that big uncle – it felt great and still does!

Letter to Mom:

I attended both your oldest grandkids college graduations. Brandon is now married and Jasmine is an entrepreneur. (You didn't miss that, did you, Mom? Generational education, legacy building and discovering both independence and interdependence.) They are making an impact in life and finding success! Mom, you should see them both now. Germon is married to a beautiful brown young lady; they are movers and shakers in dance choreography, in acting and in the Christian rap industry in California. Delece is an entrepreneur business owner in the domestic capacity. Both are thriving parents now, and doing well. So, yes, you have great-grand children! Courtney has twins; you always said we had twins on your side of the family. Cece has a beautiful daughter. Cha, is doing well, taking after you in the field of healthcare. Kar is doing well too, living out his dreams. You'd be so proud of them, Mom!

You see, my sister and I shared the same father, yet I never witnessed you treating her different or funny. In fact, I recall you doing her hair and buying her clothes; she had her own closet when she came to visit us or spend the weekend with us. Because of that, I was able to meet her mom and not feel awkward in that moment, and I thank you for that. In fact, I hugged her, because you and Dad taught us to love people, and it's not the person but humanity that we are all born with (Psalm 51:5), humanity of the mind or heart causing them to be different from you in what God might allow them to experience in their humanity.

(Con't Letter to Mom)

Because of your positive demonstration of love, it enabled me to be a gentleman to someone who easily could have hated you for marrying Dad. During that moment, the graduation out of town, my sister didn't know how I would get along with her mother; I guess she thought I'd be angry and envious towards her mom. But I only felt compassion, love and respect for her, because she was a mother too, no doubt doing all she could to be a positive example to her children and provide for them. So, thanks for showing me how to conduct myself as a gentleman and brother to my sister even though we did not grow up in the same household. Lessons like that are treasurable moments I miss about you. You were a teacher – even when you were quiet, you were teaching, demonstrating, showing us how to conduct ourselves in any situation! And in this moment, I honor you for your mothering and for giving me a lifelong bond with my sister. Continue to rest in heaven.

Looking back, the move to 539 South 73rd Street was one of the best decisions my parents made. I met my best friend and future wife and developed as a young man at that address. Around 1987, we moved from the urban core to what we would call now the suburbs. I recall not sleeping well the first week in our new home, because unfortunately, we were used to police sirens at all hours of the day and night, gunshots, people breaking into your home, etc. That first night, I remember looking out my window actually listening to crickets at night, instead of gunshots and sirens. It was weird at first, until I became accustomed to our new home. But once we settled in, we were all over that neighborhood, riding our bikes and meeting the other kids.

Transferring from Northwest Middle School to Arrowhead Middle School was somewhat of a culture shock to me. The girls liked me, and I liked them back! But this was more of an opportunity to start in sports, and of course the guys were cool – well, some were! From a cultural perspective, the teachers, administration and staff were all Caucasian, which was new to me! All my teachers at Northwest were from HBCUs. We had one African-American teacher that I can recall, Ms. Nash.

Because I had attended NWMS, I was put in reading lab, math lab and just about any other remedial program available back then. However, once I settled in and learned the system, those classes were no longer needed. You see, the stigma was that I had attended an inner-city school, and based on that, I was considered academically deficient. For some reason, that did not sit well with me back then, plus I did not want the guys and girls to see me as different academically. It was at that point that I had a decision to make: not to be a statistical story but to overcome the stereotypes and thrive.

Needless to say, I turned my grades around and started wrestling, basketball and track. I lost weight, bulked up and stepped into my teenage years lean and fit. Because of the move from 2520 Stewart to 539 South 73rd, I missed football season. But the foundation of who we were was already a part of our make-up, and we didn't even know it. For example, I was able to reinvent who I was in the suburbs and become a popular kid, a well-dressed young man and a starter in every sport I participated in.

Letter to Mom:

There are times when I find myself crying, whether it's watching an energy-charged movie or a parental moment in a movie scene. And you know Dad did not raise us to be crybabies or jelly-back men, so what I do is shake it off and keep it to myself. Unfortunately, that's how I processed your death. I buried it as a young man. That's how I dealt with the grief of losing you. My mentality or mantra became "If I could manage your death, nothing in life would or could hurt me again," which is far from the truth.

All I can do sometimes is think about my kids – your grandkids. Yes, Dee and I both had children after you passed. Dee has a beautiful girl, Chevelle. She is very smart, determined and a joy to be around – you would have loved her. Then Lorie and I had two – yep, Mom… we have two, Evin and Alana! Being there for them, especially our daughter, regardless of the situation… being in position to do all I can to ensure they are both prosperous and well cared for, without any issues in life, is of the utmost importance to us. It makes me feel dejected at times that you never had the opportunity to meet my kids or that, just like you, someday I too will leave the earth and not be there for my kids either. In fact, Chuck's kids are the last grandkids you had the opportunity to be around, to know you gave them the essences of your spirit.

In hindsight, I recall the conversation we had a few years after I graduated from college. You asked me when we were planning to have kids and if it would be soon. What I did not understand, or could even fathom, was the innocence of your motherly wisdom; you felt or knew your time with us was limited, and you felt something, but you only hinted at it. You were never pushy, nor did you articulate that directly to me. You instead let us figure it out on our own. I respect and love you for respecting my timeline and youthfulness while indirectly trying to send me a clear message ("Look, Kevin, I don't know how much longer I'll be alive, but I would like to have the opportunity to meet your kids and get to know them").

I apologize for not understanding what you were really saying to me then; but now that I'm a parent, I get it. I apologize for not understanding how lupus and diabetes affected you more than I realized, the tingling in your hands and those foot massages you requested from time to time. I am so grateful you were my mom!

Evin is an energetic, witty little man who's kind of like me in some senses. He keeps everyone laughing and is a momma's boy! Hear any parallels in this? You would have loved him as well. Evin knows about you, I made sure of it! He knows that whenever we pass the cemetery on I-70, I honk the horn three times. He has asked me several times, "Are you missing your mom?" If he only knew how my heart aches still! Alana is my little queen; there is so much I want to do for her as a father. At the start of this project (which I call journaling), she is only eight months; she is pulling up and trying to walk, and she can say "Da-Da." In fact, she is progressing so fast it's scaring me!

Mom, I know if you were still here with us, you'd have your own room in our house; Lorie and I talk about it and you often. Lorie and I both long for you. We know if you were here, we wouldn't have to worry about who to trust or whether or not other people's habits would be appropriate for our children to be around, just like you and Dad raised us. Not that we can't trust people, but we knew your heartbeat for family and kids. You would be able to teach us so much, as a young couple trying to do all we can to be the best parents in a new era of life. Basically, in this new era, anything can be rationalized as good, honorable or okay. It's a different time from what you and Dad taught us back in the '70s and '80s.

The fortunate part is, we had your funeral services recorded. Why? Because I knew at some point, there would be other grandkids you'd never know or get to see, ever! And for that reason, I knew those kids would need to have a sense of who you were, what type of grandmother they had missed out on having. Momma, your signature lemon cake has successfully been taught to your granddaughter… it lives on another generation!

The weird thing is, I tried to watch your funeral service, alone, months after your death and could not make it through the opening music and credits. I cried like a baby and had to stop the video. I never attempted to watch it again until 2020, during Covid-19 lockdown, when I was blessed to see it with your grandkids. I guess I had intentions on watching it with the kids in the future, and the Lord gave me strength to sit through it and watch it with them. We cried together this time.

Mom, I miss our friendship, going to the movies and out to dinner at Applebee's or Chili's. You showed me how to relate to females, entertain them, share a bond and establish boundaries within the constructs of a relationship with the opposite sex. Thank you. What I miss the most is "junkin." (To those who do not know what junkin means, it means going to affluent neighborhood garage sales, buying useful things others no longer needed and using them to enhance your environment or appearance. Yes, hand-me-downs.) Remember, the last thing we bought was the chandelier; it looked great in the main hallway of our first house.

Thank you for your teachings, for instilling in me confidence, humility, compassion and the mindset to be responsible for the things around me. Lorie is finally getting me to the point that I'll make the bed – you know I hated doing that and frankly didn't care if I made the bed or not prior to leaving for the day. But a lot has changed, including me. I sign out saying, I love you and won't ever forget you!

Well, by this point, I was finding my way around the new school, Arrowhead Middle School (AHMS), as an eighth-grader. Through wrestling, I met Patrick (Pat) Newman. I wrestled 150 lbs. as an eighth-grader, and Patrick Newman wrestled as our heavyweight. He was a benevolent guy, a jokester. He was already the size of a grown man; he must have weighed about 180 lbs. and stood about 5'11", while I was only about 5'9" then. Needless to say, we had to wrestle each other in practice; the only other person between us in weight was Greg Stout, and he wrestled in the 172 lbs. weight class. Later, as I got to know Pat, I learned that my dad and his mom worked together at Sunshine Biscuits cookie factory in Fairfax, Kansas.

Pat and I hit it off well. We have the same friendly manner, polite disposition and demeanor. Once we started wrestling competitively against other schools, it became real! We had to wear a singlet that felt awkward – I almost felt naked in front of the audience of onlookers. The first home wrestling meet was kind of embarrassing: an eighth-grader, wearing a singlet in front of all his peers. Plus, there was always an Eddie Haskell type guy in the audience. That guy was Alex Springfield. He always had jokes and would attempt to clown you in front of people or whenever an audience was around. Needless to say, I understood I wasn't the one afraid to expose myself to my peers in a singlet, as much he was a chump for not being able to survive the sport himself. So, I ignored his annoying behavior until basketball season. The funny thing was that once the girls heard about me and Pat Newman being in a singlet, a group of them started attending more wrestling meets. We were building a following! At the same time, all the guys stopped attending. That was my first time girls started showing a brotha some attention… smile.

Back then; we played "body" and "pencils." I learned to handle them with body before school started in the mornings. For those who don't know, body is a fair exchange of body or chest blows (with the fist), nothing above the chest. Each person would give their best body blow (fist hit to the torso) to the challenger, and then you'd have to stand still and take a body blow from them. Each person got a fair shot, unless they flinched. If you flinched, I believe the other person would get an extra body blow. Pencils was another game similar to body, only with a pencil. The point of the game was to break the opponents' pencils with only your pencil; each person got a turn, one-for-one.

There was also Carlos Fields. That was my guy! He had been in the eighth grade more than once, so needless to say, he was the eighth-grade version of Flavor Flav. He wore Adidas jogging suits and a Kangol hat and was a break-dancer and rapper. Carlos was crazy in a good way, yet a charismatic guy that everyone knew and loved. So, by now you can see the type of guys I was around. Only Pat was okay enough for my parents to allow him to come around and hang out with me. Guess my parents did not want me to be too influenced by Alex and Carlos's behavior and conduct (1 Corinthians 15:33).

Immediately after wrestling season ended came basketball season, and because I was already academically eligible, all I had to do was make the team. And, as you already know, I was competing with Alex Springfield. This guy would not go away! We competed in every facet of eighth-grade exploration: girls, sports and just being popular. Academics were not his strong suit. I was never the best at basketball (BB), but I knew how to use my body and how to position myself to get rebounds. So, I thought I would be good so long as I worked on my offense skills. I was horrible offensively, but defensively I'd knock you down. Just before tryouts, I told my dad I was trying out for BB and might need new team shoes if I made the team. My dad built us a BB goal in front of our new house; it was a project because we surrounded the goalpost with cement and a breakaway rim. It was nice! But the evergreen trees were always in the way until we pruned them back.

The day of the tryouts, a new guy got on our bus. His name was Kevin Graham. We talked on the bus, and he inquired about things at school: sports, girls and anything that would be beneficial to know, because he had just started at AHMS that day. I thought I should be the first to at least fill him in on things at my school. Kevin Graham transferred from West Middle School Jr. (WMS) as an eighth-grader just like me, and the coolest thing was that his name was Kevin too! Besides that, he lived about five or six blocks up the street from me, off 78th Street (I lived on 73rd). So, on the bus ride, I told him about BB tryouts that day. Once he got to school, I believe he called back home to get his BB shoes brought to the school in time for the tryouts. So now this dude got a chance to try out, and he made the team! We had already played a few games, and I was the starter. Alex Springfield made the team too, but he was ineligible after tryouts, so he did not get to play, even though he was good enough to have been an asset on our woeful BB team. But instead, this Kevin Graham guy made the team. I still can't remember how he made the team, because he had just about missed tryouts. Nevertheless, they gave him a chance to play, and then he became a starter too. So, now you have the first introduction of Kevin and Kevin! It was at this point that we became inseparable until junior year of college.

Kevin Graham and Patrick Newman became my close friends. We both had similar family structures: father, mother and siblings. The only difference was that Pat was an only child, so he didn't have siblings. Pat and I tried out for the track team. I can't recall if Kevin did – in fact, I don't think he was allowed to. Mr. Henry Graham was a very serious man; he made sure that Kevin and his older brother Mike did their chores and helped him with his family garden. Henry did not play with his garden work! I even remember helping Kevin and Mike once or twice, but because I was on the track team, I did not hang around there long!

Over that summer, my friendship bond with Kevin grew stronger; he was more like my twin brother. Not only did we connect because of similar upbringing and family dynamics, we both were athletes and loved girls! The only thing we had to do was get his clothing game up. So, we started working at Taco Bell on State Ave. later in high school and over summer breaks; in the

"Dotte" (a.k.a. Wyandotte County), public transportation was a joke, so we bought our own cars by sophomore year. Meanwhile, we were stacking up our gear (the urban word for clothing apparel) over the summer. You see, strong men shaped our young perspectives on life! Both our fathers were the patriarchs of the home, our mothers were the matriarchs, we regularly attended church and our parents served in leadership roles within the church.

Although we became "boys" (urban jargon for best friends), things for me remained the same freshman year, when I attended F.L. Schlagle: I played football, wrestling (did not make the BB team) and ran track. The summer before, I lifted weights in preparation for the upcoming football season and tryouts. Needless to say, I made the freshman team as an outside linebacker, but then I was elevated to JV as a freshman, along with Lawrence Mc Cluney (my cousin, a.k.a. Mack) and Sylvester Barnett. There were others who were elevated too but later became ineligible or quit because they could not take the directions and instructions from Coach Randy Westfahl (a.k.a. Coach). I learned really early to adhere to authority and follow instructions, even if you have something you thought different, and keep your mouth closed until asked to speak... Those lessons got me in with a few of the upperclassmen.

Mack and I had another cousin who was an upperclassman at Schlagle as well: my dad's brother's son, Stanford Bailey, who was a junior (two years older than me). We had grown up in church together at Lakeside C.O.G.I.C. back in our youth. Freshman year we worked together at McDonald's on 48th Parallel (which is no longer in existence). McDonald's was actually my first job, not Taco Bell, which was later in sophomore year. While working at McDonald's, I earned enough to buy my first pair of Michael Jordan shoes and later saved enough to buy my aunt's black-on-black 1980 Monte Carlo. I immediately got the windows tinted and put two 12" subwoofers in the trunk with amps and maroon-colored free air woofers to match the maroon vinyl interior of the Monte.

After having my Jordan's for two weeks, I wore them to P.E., but I changed my shoes before class because I valued their cost and wanted to keep them looking nice without any marks or scratches. After P.E. class ended, I went back to my locker to wash up and change from my gym clothes back into my street clothes, only to find my Jordan's gone. Yes, I had gotten "jacked" (urban jargon from the 1990s, meaning to get something taken from you). Believe it or not, I had forgotten that you can still get jacked at Schlagle, after moving to 539 South 73rd Street made me kind of forget the prior community I came from. Not that the inner city is all bad, but if you open yourself up, someone will take advantage of your vulnerabilities until you learn how to protect yourself and your belongings… lesson affirmed and duly noted.

So, by now I think you see where this is headed. Now that I was in high school, it was all about maturity, growth, reputation and image. I was already in sports, working and improving my clothing situation as well. Having an older brother, Chuck, I had seen first-hand that having a tight clothing game was imperative to your image and reputation as a young man back in 1987. Gangs were getting started in the community around this time as well. N.W.A., Ice Cube, the D.O.C. – the whole West Coast gangsta rap was taking form and was the music of choice back then.

Needless to say, treating girls in the fashion that the music was promoting was a total contradiction to how we, Kevin Graham and I, were raised to conduct ourselves; we were raised to be young gentlemen, not knuckleheaded thugs or gangsters.

In fact, by that time, my dad had started his own church. Love Chapel C.O.G.I.C, and it was down the street from Schlagle too, next to the baseball diamond, old 3 & 2 baseball fields, on 59th Parallel. So, now you have to factor in my image and reputation while adding P.K. to the narrative of my life. If you don't remember that acronym, it means preacher's kid. It's a thing! Not the most desirable label to carry around as my high school image and rep was forming as a young man.

It was at this point that I learned what applied discipline and supporting family truly meant. In fact, I remember so vividly, my parents and siblings had a meeting in the living room one evening. My father asked us, as his children, if we would support him in "his calling" from God to establish a new ministry. At that time, we were too young to understand the implications of our decisions; all we knew was we were going to support family regardless of what anybody else had to say or do.

So, by now you are wondering, how is this young man going to balance being a P.K., being an athlete and working a job while maintaining this new image and developing in high school? I can only say this: it was challenging and frustrating at times, living up to the Christian standards of abstinence and now being a P.K., on top of being an athlete and working a part-time job after football and wrestling practices. I was not alone, though, because I had my boy Kevin and a few other guys on the football team to hang out with. I had started hanging with some unsavory young men, but my reputation was growing more than I knew. I was starting to be introduced to upper-classmen girls and girls at other schools in KCK: Harmon, Wyandotte, Washington, Ward and Sumner.

My spirits were growing too, as I gained spiritual wisdom by night, while during the day I was about freaking the girls ("freaking" being an urban word that means getting close to girls, physically, up to and including pre-marital sex). So, yes, I was a double-minded young man (James 1:8) and image conscious. That all came tumbling down after my reputation and image became bigger than what I planned on, to such an extreme that I was humbled by God and I knew it!

I started dating a young lady (who shall remain nameless) who attended Wyandotte H.S. as a freshman. Things were getting serious enough for me to start lying to my parents about my whereabouts, sneaking over her house whenever her parents were not there or mine were working or just unaware of what I was doing. I was so interested in her that I walked in the snow over 30 minutes back into the city to her house and then back to my associate's home. (He was not a true friend anyway, because he didn't care enough about me being disrespectful to my parents and lying to them – in fact, he encouraged it.) He called me stupid for walking that far and not getting anything for it. (You do follow my insinuation, don't you? Promiscuous sex.)

Needless to say, what was brewing among the fellas from the Wyandotte football team was jealousy and hatred. There were guys who didn't even know me wanting to fight me or jump on me, and yes, there were guys from my own high school who had relatives over at Wyandotte High, so they kept fueling or instigating the issue by passing rumors and fictitious messages from Schlagle to Wyandotte High School football players. Before you knew it, I was threatened and told not to come to the game that Friday night or expect to get jumped on. Well, because of my pride, I went to the game anyway and then decided to walk up to McDonald's west on Minnesota Ave., passing by a cemetery on a dimly lit street. The football team made good on their threat, and a few other former North West Middle school, NWM, foes and their family members joined in on the whole thing – I got jumped, and there was no one around to help me fight. For the first time in my life, I actually felt alone.

After that weekend, I returned to school that Monday only to be laughed at and have my reputation/image smeared. It was a humbling experience by God. But God had to break me (John 7:43-44)! He had to teach me that "no man is an island" and everyone needs someone to be their friend or supporter. That was a trial or test, which turned into a testimony later in life.

Later that same year, I began to pray for forgiveness, because my ego had gotten so big that I got lost, becoming such a superfluous ego-driven being that I no longer knew myself. My ego was growing so big that I would lurk in the basement of the church just to meet and try to mack to the girls. From an urban perspective, to mack meant to verbally spit game or use your verbal skills to entice a girl into giving you a chance to get to know her better. Sometimes, it ended in rejection and embarrassment, while other times, she was just as interested in you as you were in her, or she was so glad someone found her pretty enough to approach and had the courage to do so. In my era, it was still incumbent on the male to approach the female, if in fact you were seduced by her attraction. And again, I was a teenager, so I was constantly caught up in the allure of young ladies... yes, plural. I loved the attention, challenge and seduction of getting to know a female, which had previously gotten me into some trouble I did not foresee or plan on. Nevertheless, I had to learn my lessons through trial and error, like most young men do.

One night during a youth revival, a minister prayed for all the youth of Kansas East Jurisdiction (a regional group of C.O.G.I.C churches that convene for a week of church). As I stood there in line waiting to be prayed for, I began to really seek God (to the unbeliever, that means asking Him to come into my heart). When it was my turn, all I remember is the minister putting his hands on my head and praying for me, and everything went black. I started shouting (praising and dancing in the spirit of the Lord) unconsciously for about 60 to 90 seconds. Once I realized it was me, having an out of body experience and that everyone else was watching me, I became ashamed – ashamed of how I had conducted myself before the presence of the Lord. Because after all, I was the football player elevated to JV as a freshman, the fly-dressed guy, up-and-coming lady-killer and, yes, P.K. Once I was humbled, I maintained a calmer demeanor. You see, I had to be humbled; I was getting out of control! Nobody could have done that for me; I had to experience it for myself.

Who was Evelyn (Thomas) Bailey? Born on August 1, 1946, she was a humble, intelligent, sincere and just woman of God. I was very fortunate to have seen the true love of a woman's transformation from a fiery, feisty, freehearted persona to the spirit of a dove. Because Evelyn Bailey (Teenie) was my mother, I witnessed her efforts, transforming and wisdom-shared daily. There was a seasoned lady, who will remain anonymous, and I witnessed my mom pour wisdom, knowledge, understanding and encouragement into this battered woman. See, in order to comprehend what I'm saying, you have to know that in the 1970s and 1980s, there was still physical whooping and abuse happening to women at the hands of their husbands – domestic violence. But my mother never had to worry herself with those issues, so she was able to encourage, support and make a positive impact on the plight of subjugated or spiritually broken women. My interpretation of "subjugated" is synonymous with "downtrodden," someone oppressed and treated inhumanely or otherwise badly by someone in power. Teenie didn't play that! You see, she was the third of 10 kids; yes, my grandparents had 10 children.

Teenie was the second girl in the Thomas family, Aunt Bessie Mae Canady was her oldest sister, and Lee (Cheetah) Thomas (born February 16, 1940) was the oldest of the Thomas household. Because of her sibling positioning, Teenie learned from her older siblings. As I told you previously, she learned how to fight, empathize, and be compassionate because of my uncle's career (one of the first African-American male cops in KCK); he rode and partnered with Harold Hooks. With that said, she learned how to read people and size up their true intentions. With those skills and a genuine personality, she did not play!

REFLECTION

One time, Teenie and my Aunt Bessie were downtown bowling in KCK off 5th street (they lived on 1111 Garfield). A few girls had animosity with Aunt Bessie, and she regulated that situation by fighting the girls… needless to say, those girls got a beat-down! This wasn't the only occasion that Teenie settled matters on the behalf of the underdog and family.

There was a group of girls in the Quindaro area (my parents were known in the Armourdale community of KCK). To paraphrase, I was told, by my mother, that there was a group of girls that initiated animosity, only this time with my mom. So, my mom and auntie went to that community. My mom fought the girls while my Aunt Bessie watched to make sure no one else jumped in… Teenie closed house again, and after it was over, they went back home. Issue resolved!

The Thomas household had three bedrooms including an attic, so Teenie shared rooms with her sisters. My Aunt Rosemary (third daughter, a.k.a. Rosie) told me of a time she was sharing rooms with my mom and my mom told her to be tidy and keep things on her side of the room; they divided the room into halves, Teenie's side and Rosemary's side. Also, I learned from Aunt Rosie that the standard of politeness and manners required all visitors and company to be served first, so whenever a visitor came to the Thomas residence for dinner, they would be served first. Grandpa – Robert Vincent Thomas, a.k.a. R.V. Thomas – laid down those types of house rules back then. He worked at the packinghouse in the West Bottoms of KC, and for his part-time hustle job, he worked a trash route to supplement income, as my grandmother was a stay-at-home mom. Grandpa took care of his house!

When my mother married my father, Charles O. Bailey, Sr., R.V. told him, "When you get tired of her or think you're gonna mistreat her, bring her back home before any of that commences." After my parents got married, my father, having come from a broken family, learned the benefits of a family: he worked with my grandpa part-time on the trash route. Ensuring my father had two jobs was a way for my grandpa to provide for his daughter, and he kept a close eye on my dad. He showed him the role of a father and how being responsible as a man can define the success of your whole family. My dad stayed underneath his wing until Grandpa's demise on July 16, 1970.

So, now that we have laid down a few fundamental things, we can build from here. As you have heard, family structure has been passed down from generation to generation, only my father's side was broken. But God! God knew His divine plan for our family, and for that reason he inserted my grandfather into my dad's life by way of my mother. This act of mentoring and my father's willingness to wisely adhere to seasoned guidance turned out to be advantageous for our family.

Together my parents both grew stronger in their marriage, partnering with other African-American families through church who were living in the same space with shared commonalities. One couple was my godparents, Harold and Barbara Johnson; Harold was an up-and-coming pastor who worked at GM, and Barbara was a homemaker and tutoring mom. She was great! In fact, she helped me early in elementary school when I first started struggling academically, and I thank her to this day for her help. People were invested in us as a household and family. Barbara served as a sounding board for my mom whenever I frustrated her by not retaining an academic concept. She would give my mom conceptual worksheets for me to work on after school to ensure I grasped the academic material being taught in class.

Harold and my father inevitably shared a lot of similarities; for example, both men were the patriarchs in their homes, had career jobs (union roles), had older brothers and other siblings, and became pastors while leading their families. So, I saw early on that a man must work, regardless of the call to lead spiritually in church. To this day, this is still a fundamental value I personally believe to be true as it relates to a man leading his personal family.

My mother worked at KU Medical Center as an LPN in the Central Service Department. She worked with a host of ladies who were striving to take care of their families too! She bonded with them and encouraged them to work through relationship/marriage issues. I had the pleasure of knowing and meeting those ladies and their family members over different periods of their hospital careers, especially on my annual trip for "take your kid to work" day at KU Medical Center. On that day, I'd get to tour the whole hospital, meet doctors and nurses, etc. I ran the halls of that hospital, and I knew the topography and layout of each hiding spot, elevator, escalator and waiting room.

My mother took a lot of pride in doing her part as a woman, mother and spouse within our home. When she later found out she would not be able to in the future, it would become an emotional drain in her mind as she pondered her full purpose as a career woman. She encouraged women and spouses to have their own respective careers and jobs. Why? From a kid's perspective, it seems to me that she wanted all women to have a degree of independence even within the structure of a marriage. She encouraged women to have a stash of cash or money put away in the event that their husband would flake on them or the marriage, so that at least she would be able to take care of herself and her kids – and that's what women did; they were caretakers and gatekeepers for their families. I even remember a particular lady who will remain anonymous. Her husband would beat her along with the kids, then send her to work with black eyes and contusions while taking her hard-earned paycheck as well. My mother was the type of woman who would care for her in the women's locker room cleaning up her wounds and give her a good woman-to-woman pep talk.

From what I could see, those types of situations frustrated her, yet during that era, women were to do as they were told without question or comment. She hated seeing anyone taken advantage of, or abused for that matter, regardless of gender, but especially women! She also counseled many women through insurmountable marriages that were either doomed from the start or flat-out misguided. She and my father also counseled many couples to work through their differences and get along. And for those ladies seeking a husband, she told them how to conduct themselves and sustain or maintain their image of a virtuous woman (Proverbs 31), and how to manage their home and budgets before we even used those terms. My mom was a teacher, although that wasn't her profession; healing the hearts of the broken was her career.

Both my parents gave so much, even when they did not have it! I recall many times when my parents would gather our clothes and give them to other mothers and families before it was considered a tax write-off. They were givers! I've overheard my parents disagreeing over tithes and budgeting finances. My dad was the worst budgeter and yet the best provider – he'd give offering before the paycheck was budgeted. He would stand up at visiting churches for offering, pledging sometimes $100 at a time (and again, this was the late 1970s through the 1980s). This was mostly when we would go to other churches for their annual church anniversary offerings. I'd watch my mom give him the side-eye before the side-eye was a thing! Please understand, this was a different era, and my mom loved and fully supported my dad to the fullest. However, she would expect, at the very least, to review the upcoming bills and financial obligations. But my dad, having been led by the Spirit, would deduce his common sense into one-dimensional divine obedience.

But the great thing was that God always came through for us as a family, despite my dad's zeal to walk in his divine purpose. Please understand, I'm not bashing my dad, the church or God's divine order or direction of any leader, but instead discussing the realities of everyday folks trying to be in alignment in their covenant with the Most High while simultaneously raising a family and being career-oriented. You see, the struggle of two committed adults, pursuing God and overcoming everything and everyone, was a thing I saw daily. The ultimate team effort! God never let us go without; we generally had enough to share or donate to others. So I feel His steps were ordered for us; if the results were that we would be okay anyway, regardless of the circumstances, then it was so. But you heard about the character of my mom, and yet she and my dad stayed married until her death. So, rhetorically, what do you call that?

I recall one time when, as a pastor, my father brought home a homeless hitchhiker – yes, a total stranger! This person was brought into our home, fed food from our refrigerator and given a place to sleep for the night. He could have killed all of us that night! Blind and unwavering faith in trusting God. Oh yeah, we had to get into our closet and give them our clothes: coats, hats, socks, pants and sweaters.

Lord knows, I'm not making my parents out to be incompetent; on the contrary, I'm sharing their willingness to help humanity regardless of their plight or situation in life, without the expectation of receiving anything in return. In its simplicity, I feel that's why we were blessed and God had favor on our lives, family and household. That was a past era, not the current one! Not that you can give and help everyone in need, but you just have to be strategic and really seek and ask God to speak to you concerning how to go about being a blessing to others as a result of your having been blessed by Him. My perspective is clear and solidified! By helping others, blessings flow back to you, but the catch is to do it as a cheerful giver. Yes, you must be glad to assist and help others. The scripture says, *"God loves a cheerful giver"* (2 Corinthians 9:7). The old adage says, "Do (*good*) unto others as you would have them do unto you." The key is to *do good*! Illustrated in 1 Peter 3:11. Mom understood the assignment and was aligned in step with her husband, and therefore, God blessed their union, household and ministry of giving, formed and fashioned out of love.

SECTION II
Trying of our Faith

In 1985, the afflictions started. This was a frustrating season of life for me, as my mother was diagnosed with lupus, which was unknown back then. Later, in the 1990s, she was diagnosed with diabetes as well. At that point, she could no longer work a career job; she tried, but there were times when she was just physically unable to perform her job duties.

Considering the values my mother grew up adhering to (and that she instilled in us), it was devastating when she learned that she could not work; not that my father or any of us would leave her without, but the mere fact that she could not *do* for herself left her feeling dependent and like a burden on us, which was not the case. Honestly, I totally understand how she felt. As a parent and husband, I'd feel awkward too, knowing that all my adult needs were dependent on the good graces of someone else. It would seem humiliating. But we were going to protect and take care of our queen, Teenie! After all, not only did she provide for us as much as she could, she taught us how to provide for ourselves. She taught us how to clean (not just clean, *deep* clean), cook, sew, bake desserts and everything else a male would not know how to do without depending on a female to do it for us. She taught us those things intentionally and for a purpose. You see, Mom had an innate sense of strong will and a desire to do, and to take it a step further, she desired to do whatever she willed herself to do with style, grace and elegance (as a woman). It is because of those attributes that I can sense the genuineness of a lady when I see or meet one. I learned from the best, right?

My mom used to make what she called macramé. (We've already established she could cook and bake – read Proverbs 31:14.) Likewise, she took orders and sold macramé to anybody interested in purchasing one (Proverbs 31:13, *"She seeketh wool, and flax, and worketh willingly with her hands"*).

Our home was clean; Mom did not allow bugs or any other type of filth to take up residence in her home (see the poem by Scott Buie at the end of this book). Every Saturday, we would clean from at least 8 a.m. (after a hearty breakfast) until sometime around 1 p.m., missing all the Saturday morning play with our friends. If they knocked on the door to ask us to come out to play, we had to tell our friends, "Hey, we can't play right now, maybe later, we're doing chores and we don't know when we're gonna be done," and shut the door. Man, we got laughed at and teased for that! But my mom was raising a standard, because most of those kids' mothers either didn't require them to clean like we did or didn't worry about keeping their house like Teenie did.

Oh, I already told you she could cook, right? Well, she could make anything from scratch, by memory! She would make oxtails and chitterlings (though only a few of us would even try chitterlings) – my mom cleaned her chitterlings three or four times "on GP," as she would say, "general principle." In my college years, when I would come home for the weekend, we would go out to Edwardsville, off K-32 Highway, and help her pick greens, and then I'd help her separate the leaves by type (collard, mustard and turnip), putting the stems in a separate bag. Then we'd wash them, season them and start the pots of water to place then inside to slow cook. We'd have smothered pork chops, liver, chicken, mashed potatoes (had to peel'em, soak'em and mash'em ourselves), fried corn (I can't tell you her recipe on that, but it was my favorite) and candied yams (which got the same treatment as mashed potatoes, only the cooking and seasoning was different based on the fact they are different potatoes).

For dessert, well, let's just say she had a natural gift for baking, and in addition to that, she later took classes to perfect her craft. She baked wedding cakes as a side hustle, just because she enjoyed seeing other folks smile, especially after they would bite into one of her cakes or pies. When I was a kid, everyone would quietly ask around at the family reunions or church picnic, "Where's Teenie's cakes or pies? What did she cook this time?" Man, we were so spoiled for great cuisine – not only did we expect it daily, we kind of took it for granted to the point that sometimes I wouldn't eat, but if I waited too long, it would be devoured.

Every now and then, we'd have "leftovers" if she made liver or something like that – you know, the foods kids generally do not like. But she would still find a way to make the meal tasty and a great dining experience. These were the opinions of people outside our home, not just us. It hits differently when others outside you home endorse and recommend you and your talents and skills to others. It's genuinely because they believe in you.

Many from the old Quindaro community would compare my mother's baking abilities to the late Eva Monroe, known throughout KCK for her baking skills (fresh berry pies, cobbler, cakes and other pastries).

I hope by now, the intangible and tangible skills of my mother have become more vivid to you. Keep in mind, she was also the first lady of my father's church. You see, she was the definition of the Proverbs 31 woman – before it became so popular, mom was that virtuous woman! The scripture tells us, *"A wise women builds her home…"* (Proverbs 14:1).

Well, it became apparent that Mom could no longer stay healthy and work full time. Luckily, at this same time (1986), my dad was asked to step into a supervisor role at Sunshine Biscuits. Timing is everything, and this was perfect timing. My oldest brother had just graduated in 1985 and started working in the Fairfax area. So, in regards to timing, Chuck graduated first and got a full-time job, then Dad was promoted to supervisor, and I was a freshman in high school and working as well. So, between her boys, Dad, Chuck and me, we all worked to cover expenses and ensure that Mom wanted for nothing.

But as I said earlier, from her upbringing, it was not in her to just sit and not make any financial contributions. So, she utilized her skills and talents by making cakes, and that became her side hustle. Although she was not working, she developed her natural talents for baking by taking classes at the local vocational school to enhance her cake-decorating skills, and she earned her certification as a professional bakery and dessert expert. Again, she was finishing what she started, being that demonstration of tenacity. That developed into the ultimate hustle, as she began taking orders to make birthday, wedding and special event cakes. Throughout my collegiate experience, she allowed me to use her car so that I would have a reliable vehicle to be able to come back home whenever necessary. Even though she had nothing to give, she still gave... her own vehicle! Everyone in our household was being stretched beyond their comfort zones in order to keep everything flowing for the good of the family.

After over 30 years of successful marriage, the female vultures started coming out. The enemy started in on Dad first: a particular female on his job became infatuated with him. She threw herself at him, and when he refused to engage with her shameful shenanigans, she proceeded to make false allegations against him at work. Now, here is how God had our family's back! The other workers and subordinates in this union work environment renounced her claims on my dad's behalf. Not only did they do that, the ladies who knew my dad, our family and my mom personally took it a step further and began to watch his back at work... even though he was their boss.

Now, please understand, because he was in leadership for an organization and allegations were being made against him, the company had to do their due diligence and document everything, as well as apply pressure on him with production expectations and work-related performance issues. Once this all went down, God started working, and my dad's union coworkers began to work harder to dispel not only the false allegations but the performance issues as well. It got so bad that organizational leadership would take his personnel from him and reassign their jobs in the act of production – pull them off their jobs without covering the job with a relief person and without the area supervisor's knowledge.

So, there was a concerted effort to sabotage Dad and make him seem guilty by any means necessary. It did not work! In fact, Dad prayed harder, we prayed harder and we had an army of prayer warriors intercede on our family's behalf. There was a company event held by leadership and the union, and the other ladies formed a spiritual hedge of protection around Mom, because they knew her prior to her sickness and still appreciated her for the woman she had transformed into.

These stories are not made up, but are true accounts I witnessed through my maturation within the Bailey home. Because we were such a private family, we never openly shared any of our trials or tribulations, not because we did not want to be a testimony to those needing to be ministered to or blessed, but because telling all your business was not how we were raised. Sharing these accounts even now is hard for me to do because of the fallout. In fact, we were told as kids, "What goes on in the Bailey home stays in the Bailey home." If an adult has a question to ask you, refer them to your parents. In other words, do not try to circumvent the parents by pumping the kids with questions for internal information. To this day, I'm very confidential with my information. Nothing personal towards anyone, but that's just how I was raised; I do not just share my business with folks. In fact, my uncle nicknamed me "Secret Squirrel" because I have the ability to bury information and never share it. As I get older, I really cannot even recall certain things.

After graduation in 1991, it was time to go off to college. I was intent on going to an HBCU; after all, I grew up watching *A Different World* as a teenager. Plus, all my prior teachers at Northwest Middle School had attended HBCUs. Because of my athletic ability in high school, I was able to earn an athletic scholarship to go off and play football. Although I had a scholarship offer to go to Fort Hays State University (FHSU) for wrestling, I elected to play football instead. I just could not see myself attending college and not being able to eat because I had to make weight. Starving in high school was somewhat inevitable (given my commitment to sports and wrestling), but why make a conscious choice to attend college on a scholarship that would have required you to intentionally starve? That made no sense to me at all! Especially when I could make a choice by playing football, which meant I could attend college with my best friends, cousin and other high school teammates, and not have to starve. Furthermore, FHSU is in western Kansas – why would I choose to not only starve away from home but move to Hays, Kansas? Sorry, that option was not for me!

So, in 1992, after graduating early from Butler County Community College in three semesters and summer school sessions with an Associate of Art in General Studies, with GPA of above 3.0, I had my eyes set on going to the University of Arkansas at Pine Bluff (UAPB) with my cousin Lauretta. I had earned an academic scholarship after BCCC to attend any college or university of my choice. My dorm application was complete, transcripts were forwarded and housing was being arranged. The relationship I had with my then-girlfriend and now wife was being manipulated, to say the least. I was in a long-term relationship with her and working towards engagement, in addition to being a full-time student, playing football, having a work-study job in the library and working off campus at a telemarketing job to pay for an engagement ring. However, my mom asked me to stay closer to home for college, because she was not feeling well and was having a lot of tests being run on her to understand what lupus was, only to be told later that she had become diabetic from taking Discovery Lupus medication and from her past A1C levels. All of that was added pressure.

To honor Mom, I made the decision to attend Emporia State University (ESU) instead of UAPB. At the graduating ceremony in Emporia, KS, I walked with a business degree, and upon receiving that certificate; I immediately walked it to my mom and presented it to her. While my girlfriend, dad, brothers, grandmother, aunts and uncles were there to watch me put my degree in her hands, my degree was a testament to my mom's sacrifices to see me through. In spite of everything, she made sure I completed my mission as an undergraduate. At that time, she said, "You did good, son!" That became my mantra in life, to *"do good."*

SECTION III

ALL THINGS WORK TOGETHER

Life as a Bailey man was trying, and it still is, more so because of the generations before me. Bailey men have long been synonymous with being great, sturdy and stately men; men who worked hard and took care of their families, responsibilities and obligations in life. In short, we're known as "God-fearing men," men of sport, men who overcome odds and men who are distinguished. I know that every Bailey man, currently and in times past, has been and continues to be responsible for taking care of their families, kids, wife and work obligations.

Things changed from my great-grandfather's generation to my dad's – yes, I left a generation out. You see, as a child, my dad stayed with our great-grandfather, Leonard Milton Bailey, Sr. After not growing up with both parents and having spent limited time with his mother for contentious family reasons, he did not meet his biological father until he was 25 years old (*Grandpa Clifford*), after he had his first son and had been married for several years. Clifford Colum was my grandfather's name. No exaggerating, he was a serviceman, now buried in Leavenworth cemetery, and a true pimp – he ran women on South Benton for years. My parents gave us the occasional pleasure and opportunity to meet and spend time with him, but not too often (1 Corinthians 15:33).

REFLECTION

One day, my parents had some business to attend to and had no loved one or friends available to watch us. So, my mom agreed, against her motherly judgment, to allow us to stay with my grandfather. During our stay with him, we hung out on the porch, on the sidewalk and inside his apartment. After lunch we took a nap, but I woke up early and witnessed my grandfather scold a young woman and send her on her way… back to work! He was never physically abusive, but verbally and psychologically he owned their minds. I was too young to really put it all together at the time, but we just never spent any more time with Grandpa unattended for influential reasons.

Watching my dad demonstrate his faith in everyday living as I grew was the best thing I ever could've seen as a young man. Many times as parents, we do our kids an injustice by not allowing them to see us go through struggles in life and how we as their parents cope and process through situations. Not that your kids need or want to see their parents go through struggles in life, but they need to see your faith in motion and not just lip service – use discretion! My point is, they need to see the God in us, and to see us processing through heartaches, sadness, disappointment and all of the above. Perhaps that's why I was blessed to see my parents take it to Him in prayer – they didn't tell everybody (friends, family, etc.), they took it to Him for resolution and clarity. But it's through those lenses of struggle that we can see how it's in the trying of our faith that humanity's failures transcend to God's divine plan for success in your life. It is imperative for modeling to occur in our life daily – after all, that's how we learn and teach others. Seeing my dad making divine decisions in life taught me how to be an effective husband and man. And I'm not perfect! Truth be told, we are all flawed; the point is, how much is witnessed, or how much can we cover up to reduce the exposure?

I've witnessed my dad get spat upon at work; when I heard that, all of us siblings were ready to fight! We were planning to go find this co-worker of his. But God! You see, in my mind, how I would have handled that is just give him a "one-hitter-quitter" – a single blow and he's taking a nap, right? Wrong. My dad was wise enough to report and allow his employer to handle it. These days, that would be called "workplace violence," even though it was warranted and just to do, in my young eyes. See,

Dad knew he had to protect his job more so than his image and reputation. As a result of that type of longsuffering on the job, he was elevated to leadership, revered by his co-workers and earned his retirement. Thirty-eight years of work at the same place – that in and of itself is a testimony.

You see, my godfather, Pastor Harold Johnson was the same way: he too worked at Ford and retired. Those were the type of men I was around as a little Bailey boy: men who worked, in addition to being called to ministry to pastor. They did not lean on the cross to take care of their families; they left an impression on me (Genesis 3:19).

Earlier as youth in church, we were known as "those Bailey boys." Why was this a thing for us? I don't know. But because of prior generational stereotypes from my great-grandfather's generation, we were labeled as hard workers, responsible men and family-oriented… as well as men you could possibly overlook because they are content and not ambitious. Wrong! None of us are naïve enough to believe that, right? Why do you think I've been so determined to overcome these foolish stereotypes as a young man and be the achiever I was raised to be? Furthermore, the men in my family shaped the community I grew up in. They had a rock quarry business, sold fruits and berries on 38th State at the Farmers Market and helped build the dam at Wyandotte County Lake, which still stands today. Bailey men did things like this, way back up to now.

It is for this reason that I have always done all I can not to disgrace or embarrass my parents, instead honoring them daily by being a responsible man, father, son, brother and husband. My philosophy is simple: if I can avoid embarrassing drama in my life, then that's more time I have on my hands to reach and strive for honorable achievements. That's why I insist on being a productive citizen. Not that I'm a "goodie two shoes," but I honestly try to *do good*, though even in our best attempt we'll struggle. The Bible says that even when you *do good*, evil is present (Romans 7:21). I choose to *do good* daily. Let me tell you something, I've seen my dad choose to *do good*, even when being tempted, threatened and mistreated. As a kid, you don't understand why your parents, Mom and Dad, would purposely take "L's," losses. What I did not know is that this was for a more divine rationale that I did not have the spiritual maturity to comprehend at the time.

REFLECTION

True story: one time while driving west on State Avenue in KCK, we were all in the car stuck in traffic off 38th Street when a biker on a Harley Davidson (along with his entourage) purposely held up traffic by not moving forward after the light changed. My dad blew his horn, and the Caucasian biker got off his Harley-Davidson bike, walked back to our car and started scolding my dad through the window of the driver's seat. His only options were to get out the car and fight them or to roll the window up completely. He chose the latter of the two, yet the biker spat on the window as if he was spitting on my father. Dad kept calm in that situation, and it defused itself. However, had he gotten out the car, what could have happened in front of his family? That could have been criminal, I'm sure.

In the end, I can only say that God knows and possesses the plan for divine order! He knew, by His divine plan, that taking our mom would benefit us long term, yet keeping our father here with us would be just as divine. Why do I say that? Because our mom was wise beyond her years, yet God still knew we needed our biological father to stay with us longer as a shoulder to lean on and help us overcome some of the other male things we'd need to mature and grow further as Bailey men. In that same vein, our bond as father and son has strengthened, and I've been able to continue to learn how this fathering process needs to go. Keep in mind, my father did not grow up with his biological father living under the same roof, yet he stayed with my great-grandfather until he was of age to work on a job. Had it not been for my great-grandpa's standing in those gaps, my dad would not know how to develop young boys to manhood and fatherhood, knowing what a responsible husband looks like. Having him in our lives is God's divine will and strategic order manifesting in our lives.

Praise be to God, my father was fortunate to be able to "reverse the curse": in one generation, he has been able to become the father he never had growing up and demonstrate being a positive brother to us and to his siblings. Just think, what if my dad had stayed with my grandfather? Would he be an active, effective father now? Would he have learned the necessary lessons in life to teach his children, nieces and nephews? Only God knew, and He orders his steps – thank you, God!

Within my dad's life, I've witnessed him officiate both his father's and mother's funeral services. In fact, he even buried his dad in one of his personal suits. Of his siblings, he officiated his eldest brother's services and spoke at his sister's funeral. In short, he has a tremendous amount of strength, and as his biological legacy, we all have absorbed an abundant amount of that strength and confidence merely by being around him throughout our lives. He retired after working for 38 years at Sunshine Biscuits, having earned his GED while I worked there. I witnessed my mother encouraging him through that whole process; even when he saw no real need to earn it, Mom made sure he completed his educational goals. See, she was a finisher and closer.

As previously mentioned, my dad grew up under the leadership of my great-grandfather. Interestingly enough, he grew up with two brothers – yes, my great grandfather had to put up with three young adolescent males under one roof. He also had two sisters by my grandfather, Clifford, but they lived in separate homes. Growing up, my dad witnessed both my uncles being made to fistfight one another for the sport of it, while my great grandfather looked on and encouraged it. Consequently, my dad never allowed us to bicker or even sound like we were arguing or thinking about fighting. In fact, he's actually raised his fist at my brother and me because the conversation sounded like we were going to fight each other; he cannot stand family not getting along and loving one another.

The number three and multiples of three are very symbolic in our lives. Dad had a daughter and three boys, and my mother was the third oldest in her family. I grew up with three siblings: two brothers and my sister. My mother passed on 3/19/00 at 6 p.m. I have only been a member of three churches in my lifetime: Lakeside C.O.G.I.C, Love Chapel C.O.G.I.C and now Concord Fortress of Hope Church, Baptist by denomination.

Speaking of denomination, my mother grew up Baptist and my father grew up Pentecostal. Although my upbringing was very Spirit filled, on occasion, we'd visited my great-grandparents church, Tabernacle Baptist Church under the leadership of Pastor Wheeler. It's the only pink church I've ever known in my life. It was always intriguing to visit their church, merely because although we both worshipped and praised God, believing in the Father, Son and Holy Spirit, it was different. As a child, I remember seeing the deacons and ministers lead worship/devotion service, only to see them outside after those segments of the service smoking on the church steps or in the parking lot. I could never understand that, especially with your body being a temple. I learned a great deal of my Christian faith while going to a Pentecostal church, but there was preferential treatment at times, based on your last name or how much money you donated, at least at the district level. Those are a few church experiences as I matured in to a young man. Overall, we had a great church family throughout Kansas East Jurisdiction, under the leadership of William H. McDonald.

My personal development has been unique, at least the way I see it. I was born on Friday, September 29, 1972, at 6:18 p.m. The first home I can remember was Victory Hills Apartment Complex. I must have been around one or two years old, around the time I was able to walk. We stayed on the top floor of the complex, while my mother's girlfriends stayed on lower levels. My oldest brother (Chuck) and I had a blast! When it rained or we could not go outside to play much, we'd run the hallways of the apartment complex, ringing residents' doorbells and then running down the hall or upstairs to hide. It was fun the first few times, until our parents found out what we were doing when one of Mom's girlfriends snitched on us. If memory serves me correctly, it was Mae-Francois. She carpooled to work with Mom; they both worked at KU Medical Center during that time.

After living there several years, our parents opted to move back into the city, 2520 Stewart, which is where my growth continues. While I was at Chelsea Elementary, my mom felt it was time for me to learn how to swim, so she enrolled me in a YMCA swimming class. This was a changing point in my life! My mother packed my bag on the first day, but she forgot my swimming goggles. So, after school, we all got on the school bus and got dropped off at the 8th Street YMCA in downtown KCK. Once we were dropped off at the front door, we headed to the locker room to change into our swimming gear. I'm sure that's when I realized I did not have my goggles.

After we got dressed for swimming class, the coach yelled for everyone to clear the locker room and enter the swimming pool area. Once we all assembled in the pool area, he allowed us to get into the water to play around and get comfortable. Then, after 5 to 10 minutes of playing around, he yelled for everyone to get out of the pool and go to the opposite end. I reluctantly got out of the pool and went over to the far end, as I was instructed to do, and once I got there, we were all instructed to stand at the edge of the pool. Again, I followed the coach's instructions out of respect, as I was raised to do.

Then the coach told us he would blow his whistle and we were to jump into the water and begin swimming. Once the coach blew the whistle, everyone dove in and started swimming – except for me. I stood there, leery of his instructions, because after all, the sole purpose for me to get swimming lessons was to learn how to swim, not to try to swim without lessons. So, after the coach realized I was still standing there and not in the water, he blew his whistle at me again and again… and I just looked at him. Then he marched towards me and shouted at me to jump into the pool. I reluctantly complied: I jumped in (without my goggles) and started mimicking everyone else, paddling my arms and flutter-kicking my feet.

That end of the pool was 8 to 10 feet deep, yet I continued swimming – or at least what I thought was swimming. One very important thing, if you haven't noticed: I forgot to breathe. So, I proceeded to open my eye to see if I had made it to the moderately shallow area of the pool yet, only to attempt to touch down on the bottom of the pool and not connect. Immediately, I panicked, because not only was I out of breath, I could not see, and the chlorine began to burn my eyes. It was bad! The swimming coach had to use the pole stick to pull me out. He yelled at me and sent me down to the shallow end, telling me, "Don't leave that area of the pool until instructed to." I was confused, to say the least; after all, the sole purpose of taking swimming lessons was to learn how to swim, not to jump in and prove my inability by almost drowning. That was preventable, in my opinion as a kid.

After that negative experience, I never swam in pools or bodies of water that were over four feet deep, until I had a son – yes, Mom, your grandson. Once we had him, I did all I could to position him to become a better swimmer than me, including lessons. At the age of four, he was enrolled in a swimming class for toddlers; the thing was, at the time, I was just watching from the stands. Here's the intriguing thing, though: upon self-reflection,

I saw that I was actually being hypocritical by requiring him to be able to swim when it was proven that I could not. So, Mom, I enrolled in private swimming lessons. My swimming coach was a cool lady, Krista, from the baby boomer generation. She was very poised, understanding and just pushy enough to require that I set personal goals to achieve. After six or seven sessions, I was confident enough to at least go to the 14-foot end of the pool; this took over 30 years to overcome. Yet I met my goals, and by the end of the 10 lessons, both my son and I were confident enough in ourselves to swim in the deep end together. Mom, it was so liberating!

As I've matured in life, I've noticed that adults, kids and all people can have a tendency to stop short of achieving their goals or overcoming their fears by not completing the process. I overcame my fears as a result of not wanting to be that helpless parent around water, pools or any water activity and be unable to help our kids. In fact, my desire (burden) to be the best parent I could be overshadowed my fears. Mom, you would have been proud of me. Not only did I overcome my water phobia, I spoke with our pastor and we started a swimming program and partnership between our church and the local school district's sporting directors to offer discounted swimming lessons to those in the church who did not know how to swim or wanted to learn how to be safer during water activities. It turned into a water safety program extended to members of the church community. As a group leader within our church, I was able to share my testimony with those in the swimming program in 2014 and encourage them to be the best swimming coaches and water safety instructors possible, making a positive difference simultaneously! *Do good!* Right.

SECTION IV
Culmination of it all

Summer traveling was always adventurous! Mom, every summer you and Dad did your best to make sure I had the opportunity to travel somewhere, whether it was family vacation, Christian camp or football camp. I traveled; we all traveled. I thank you both for putting that spirit of exploration and adventure in me and my siblings. This helped greatly, especially now as a parent. Those same values and principles are being shared with your grandkids today. It's amazing seeing your kid's eyes light up the first time they get on a plane and fly; from the takeoff to the landing, it's an exciting experience. I recall the first time we took our son to the restroom on a plane. There wasn't enough space for both of us to be in there simultaneously. It was quite odd, standing outside the small bathroom door, explaining to a toddler what to look for and not to touch anything! People do different stuff on planes in bathrooms for some reason, right? It was horrifying to me! How did you do it? I know I was your curious child… I can't imagine. Thank you for your patience. I see now that parenting is an exploratory art form, hodgepodge with: coaching, mentoring, (Parental) job rotation, instructional and on the job training, OJT.

I recall often listening on you and Sister Barbara's (my Godmother) conversations. Honestly, I listened in on them all the time. I learned a lot from listening in on adult conversations. I felt your concern for me as I struggled academically in elementary school. Yes! I listened in. I heard all those whole conversations. I was determined to not make you feel embarrassed, frustrated or concerned. Honestly, I tried very hard at school. I appreciated the tutoring, and the workbooks and academic worksheets and workbooks Sister Barbara gave me. I acknowledge that perhaps I was a knucklehead and just hated reading, math and anything I personally didn't enjoy. But you'd be surprised by the peer influences I dealt with at school and overheard the teachers talking about. Those things motivated me like you wouldn't believe… because they doubted me! I soon proved them all wrong, and I knew I had to do it for myself, and by myself, without your help.

Christian camp helped tremendously! What it did was give me overall perspective on how to incorporate your teachings, values and behaviors from a distance without you looking over my shoulder. (I struggle with this often now as a parent; we live in a different era now. The '70s and '80s were different!) I had to rely on that teaching while functioning among my peers. But I noticed a few things: either these other dudes/young men didn't have mothers who taught them like you taught us, or they didn't listen. As you already knew, kids do behave differently around parents than they do without them.

I recall going to two Christian camps during my youth: Circle-C and L Bar C Ranch, which were both operated by Youth for Christ Ministries, off Stateline. I know you were terrified to let me go, but as many dads do, Dad encouraged you to allow us to explore and grow as teenage young men from the urban core of KCK. I actually embraced and enjoyed the experience. We had prayer, three meals daily (all you can eat… I maintained my manners, though – I never pigged out or acted as though I had no "home training") and Bible study twice each morning prior to lunch (plus group worship and evening worship). They offered a variety of activities: water slides, horseback riding, ATV riding, canoeing, basketball, baseball, pool, ping-pong, arts and crafts, etc.

I enjoyed the rural exposure; it was quite different from the normal neighborhood sounds. The sky was clear – not as if our skies were cloudy, but I just noticed there was a slight difference. I can't really put my thumb on it; it was just different. Circle-C Ranch seemed hot, not a lot of shade. As a black young man, I didn't feel I needed a tan… although I'm sure you noticed a complexion change once I returned home after being away for seven days. I recall Circle-C Ranch being just outside Edgerton, KS, south on I-35. Really, it was only 50 minutes from KCK, yet close enough for me to feel away from you all. It allowed me to grow in some areas I likely needed to grow in anyway, so thank you for giving me that experience! The only thing is that I just wished there were more kids there who looked like me.

L-Bar-C Ranch was the coolest of the two campuses, facility-wise; it was nestled in the hills and valleys of La Cygne and Stanley, KS. Once you all dropped me off, that long walk to the cabin and check-in was a long process. I was hungry and worn out afterwards. Needless to say, I slept like a baby that night. Breakfast was always great, again, all you can eat with special themes each day: pigs in a blanket, Belgian waffles (with whipped cream, strawberries and other fruits), all the milk you could want, orange juice, apple juice, etc. The only part I didn't like was KP. I didn't know what KP was when I got there; obviously, I had no frame of reference to lean on at that time. I soon found out it merely meant "Kitchen Patrol." Essentially, you're doing chores in the kitchen – pans, pots, plates, cups and silverware. Heck, I never was good at dishes! (Even in my earlier childhood, on Stewart. Tracy remembers how we worked it – we had a deal.) I thoroughly enjoyed riding horses and ATVs. Heck, I even tried canoeing – didn't care for it, but the mere opportunity to try something new was refreshing, so I thank you for those experiences. Little did I know you all were preparing me for something different than my teenage experiences would have allowed me to discover.

Then there was the football trip to Chicago with Fellowship of Christian Athletes (FCA), with Ron Freeman. Turns out his son was, Josh Freeman, who played quarterback at K-State. This was yet another opportunity for growth, development and independence as a young male growing up in the urban core. It was a childhood dream! Why, you probably ask? My cousin and I were around the same age; we always played football together at the annual family reunion. Yet we never had the pleasure of playing on the same team! See, he lived in Kansas City, MO, and I lived in Kansas City, KS. Two very distinct cities, yet separated only by a river. They are known as sister cities, like Minneapolis and St. Paul, MN. Needless to say, we never saw a difference as kids, and we always relished the opportunity to spend time together, whatever the circumstances.

You see, we had life plans – we agreed on a plan for each other for life! We agreed we'd make it to the NFL (and become star running backs), marry light-skinned women (colorism at an early age), take care of our families and never become drunks! See, we grew up seeing our uncle drunk often. We loved him anyway; we just knew he had a drinking problem. Like most kids discover about family members in their youth, we didn't know what caused it, we only saw the aftermath, and as kids, we vowed we'd never become drunkards. Funnily enough, we were so naïve that we thought if we attended the same school and played on the same football team, we'd have a shot to make our plans a reality. We knew as kids, as cousins, that we had enough determination to will our plans into reality. Manifestations at an early age. A reality that would lift up our families to riches and good living! I know that was a little far-fetched and naïve, but nevertheless, we thought up our life plan as kids… how could it ever work?

Well, this FCA trip with my cousin and his childhood teammate was becoming a reality with FCA. Ron Freeman was our chaperone for the drive to Chicago. We stayed in the dorms for five to seven days. This was my first chance to experience competition from across the country; this too was an eye-opening experience. At that time, I played linebacker, on defense, or so I thought! But there was this kid that everyone was raving about, a highly acclaimed tailback/running back named Calvin "Endzone" Jones. I had never heard of this guy before the football camp. He would later sign to play for the Nebraska Cornhuskers as a running back, and he became a Husker star.

This trip to Chicago was fun! We even rode the L commuter train. My mother had no clue I was this free and walking the streets of Chicago. We walked a few streets and quickly learned the street codes. If you wore a hat, it could only be white, and it had to sit in a normal position on your head and not turned to either side or backwards. Each position had a meaning; we were told the position of your hat on your head meant you were a member of a particular neighborhood gang. Needless to say, we were chaperoned when we walked to the neighborhood corner convenience store. The main point was that my cousin and I were together, away from home doing what we loved, and we didn't have parental oversight (oh yeah, wasn't that the purpose of Ron Freeman?). We did not care! We were together! We never cut up – too bad.

We loved even having the mere opportunity to play the game; being together, alongside each other as cousins meant the world to both me and him, especially as young men, and it fueled hope we'd be a dynamic duo if we played together. Wishful thinking, I know. But we were able to dream as kids, and dream big we did! After all, dreams don't cost anything, right? As kids, we freely dreamed! We prayed and talked to God, because we were taught that He's *"the author and finisher of our faith"* (Hebrews 12:2), and we had big faith that He would bring our dreams to fruition!

Sophomore year, I was fortunate enough to attend football camp yet again, at the University of Nebraska–Lincoln (UN), Home of the Cornhuskers. At that time, legendary coach Tom Osborne was the head coach. There were several F.L Schlagle Stallions teammates who attended this camp too, along with another cousin of mine! Marlon Mitchell and Lawrence Mc Cluney. We stayed in camp for a week together, which was typical back then. At this point, being away from my family was considered routine; after all, I'd gone away from them each summer since seventh grade. I felt they weren't worried about me… that I knew of. So, being away was good for me, from a maturity perspective as well as honing my craft at football.

During this time, the Cornhuskers' weight room was under construction; they were set to build the biggest weight room and rehabilitation facility in college history. The rumor was that they were planning to have the weight room stretch the length of the stadium underneath the stadium seats. Calvin "End-zone" Jones had all the coaches' attention again. Apparently, that nickname had to do with his knack for scoring touchdowns. The coaching staff drooled over him and courted him as a potential recruit to attend Nebraska. Funnily enough, he was a National All-American at the halfback position. The only other halfback I knew of with high school buzz and clout was Haromma Dickerson from Harmon High School.

Haromma was a bruising halfback; he would "truck" defenders (run through and over them) in games. We played Harmon at their homecoming in the '90s. Haromma had been successfully running to the left side of our defense for the majority of the game. Guess who played on that side of the defense: my best friend. He would only run to my side, the right side, and he did it twice that night. The first time was a counter-play with lead blockers pulling from his left side of the offensive line. The first play, I used the "Swim" technique I learned from summer camp at UN. I busted through his line shucking and swimming past linemen to tackle him for a loss in the backfield. They tried that one more time with the same result, and they never tried me again that night! We won that game! My cousin "The Toe" (Stacy Thomas) kicked the winning field goal, and the final score was 14 to 11. It was a 49-yard field goal, almost a Kansas state record. (He would later break that state field goal record with a 52-yard kick.)

At one point during my college years, I traveled to University of Arkansas at Pine Bluff to visit my cousin, Lauretta It was an exciting time for me. After all, I had recently crossed into my fraternity! She and I were thick as thieves as teenagers. She came to pick me up from the Little Rock Airport, we went back to campus and I stayed the night at her house... slept on the floor but had a great time! That next morning, we traveled to Grambling State University in Louisiana for "Spring Fest," which I had never heard of before. That was a great time too. We listened to Domino on the trip down there. He had a song at the top of the charts that year: "Here we go, here we go..."

After being on an HBCU campus, I was hooked! That summer, I put in my transfer paperwork (transcripts) and had my course schedule, dorm assignment and financial aid lined up. All was set to go, until Mom asked me to select a school closer to home... even though I was on an academic scholarship and tuition was paid. Her rationale was, "If I need you to come home during the semester, you can't without having to purchase a plane ticket." So, I agreed to stay closer to home, and Mom gave her car to me for traveling purposes. And with that car, did I ever travel! I would leave the campus of Emporia State University (ESU) on Friday after classes (or sometimes Thursdays) just to get out before everyone would leave for the weekend. ESU was and still is a "suitcase" college, meaning each week, I would leave for the whole weekend only to return Sunday night or early Monday morning, grab some breakfast and run to class across campus.

Once I found a job, I would stay in town on weekends. I worked at The Farm, Inc., an emergency facility for juveniles and minor offenders. After teaching youth in Sunday school, being a big brother, paraprofessional and subbing, I was equipped to encourage, motivate and inspire young people to dig deeper and make a difference!

Earlier in my college experience, let's just say I made a few bad decisions that resulted in me being put on paper. I'll never forget the embarrassment of walking down Commercial St. (the main street) to get to my PO's office for monthly check-ins. I'd go inside, sit and wait to be seen by the PO officer. From time to time, he'd ask how you were doing. I kept my words few and answered his questions so I could promptly leave. Sometimes he would ask me if he needed to test me Urine Analysis (UA) exam, and I'd answer, "Test me if you like." He eventually did, and I passed. After that, he was easy to get along with. Once he found out I was not some 'knucklehead" but a respectful young man, I had no issues with him, and my probation cycled out without any issues. The key here is the unwavering support I had from family. You all taught us that things will not always go your way, but be of good cheer and know "joy cometh in the morning" (Psalm 30:5). That faith carried me! To endure hardness, as a good soldier... except he strives lawfully (2 Timothy 2:3-5).

Being on probation was especially challenging. If it were not for you, Mom, I would have been locked up in jail. Youthfulness and inexperience in life can be very detrimental if not guided through properly by parents and loved ones who believe in you, through rough times with a seasoned, mature and wise counselor. How did you do it, Mom? You guided me spiritually and mentally through times I knew I should not have shown you in my life... I thank you! You did not let me slide in my error; you allowed correction to fall on me, but not the full weight of it. You taught to me to be responsible and claim the error in my ways.

As you taught me, I prayed in secret, with a sincere heart and soul, for I believed He would hear my "faintest cry (and answer them by-and-by)" – yes, I still remember the song the old saints taught us. Oddly enough, they do not sing those old country songs anymore; perhaps they were not taught the things we were taught. That's not an indictment or criticism, it's just my own personal justification for why others may not know what we knew or have been taught the way we were. I used to hate being the kid at prayer meeting on weeknights while all my peers were at home watching TV, playing Atari games, riding their bikes and just being kids. Our normal was different as PKs.

My collegiate endeavors were challenging! I worked so hard to obtain a goal, and for the first time in life, I was defeated, and it hurt. Honestly, I was not prepared academically, which I found out early in community college. The hard part was asking for help and knowing who would see the fact that I was struggling academically, despite my circumstances. Once I understood those struggles, I could develop a plan of attack to overcome the shortfalls. My undergraduate motto was "Nobody is going to help me but me." In other words, whatever I had to do to achieve and overcome obstacles, only I could advocate, motivate and encourage myself.

Many times, this is the African-American experience and mindset: it's in the failures that you learn the most. Pressure makes diamonds. You either rise to the occasion or accept defeat, turn away and mope in your failure. I chose to rise! I wasn't doing it for me – instead, Mom, I chose to rise to honor you! I always knew you were so strong, only you were harnessed in your delivery of that strength. You were an observer of all; nowadays they call it being a "people-watcher." You knew the pulse and temperature of whatever room you entered, and sometimes even before you entered them. You had an amazing gift of discernment. When people dealt with you, they knew you were sincere and genuine. Everyone appreciated that about you. Even to this day, your true friends think of you when we run into them out in public, and they still say, "She was a special lady." These are not things I or anyone else would have to invoke folks to say about you; it's that they felt this way about you for some reason. They can recall moments when you made them feel special, as only Teenie could. You knew how to pray, tarry, and that was the gift that was bestowed on you! I still believe each person has a particular gift designed to enhance the human experience we call life, and you found yours. Others do not and some never even think they are capable of learning what gift they have, but you did, and you worked it for your good. I learned from that daily.

Speaking of gifts, I'll never forget the smile on your face the day I graduated from ESU. I remember the sacrifices you made for me, giving me your car (the maroon Nissan Stanza), the money you saved up from making cakes, how you would discreetly put it into my hand with a smile or wink; I appreciated that. So, when I finally earned my degree, we earned it together, and I had no problem giving it to you. In fact, I was honored to present you with it because of your sacrifices. I recall putting that degree in your hands – the pride and grace you showed was worth it all! I just had to honor you in that moment. And to know we share, together, a completed journey of academic challenges that were made possible through your sacrifices and dedication was the greatest blessing I could return to you as a son. I'm sure I'll have an opportunity to share this with young men some day. Love you, Mom!

A mother is the original cheerleader for a male, unequivocally. She is the closest genuine woman on earth who will unapologetically support you, while loving you through your journey and mistakes in life. *Never* disrespect her. Love her and honor her in all you do, just to see her smile. That's not a lot to ask of a son.

Letter to Mom:

Yesterday was your birthday, August 1. I did not call any of my siblings, not because we've fallen out, but because I just really did not feel like doing anything. I was neither sober nor sad. It was merely a day of relaxing and reflection. What does that mean? This bond we have as mother and son, in your divine absence, lends itself to how I choose to keep you afresh and in my heart, so that I do not do the one thing you asked me not to do. It is in that same vein that I must... Not that I'll forget you or attempt to replace you, but that I may continue to honor you all the more through my daily sacrifices as a parent (as in the Ten Commandments, Exodus 20:12). Just as you taught me, now I must live it by the example you demonstrated.

You know, you were a very wise soul, Mom. You requested something from each of us. The request you asked of me has been noted, but what did you request of Dad? (To the reader: that will be revealed later in another chapter... keep reading.) Lastly, what did you request of my other siblings? You've always had a way of laying or making an impression on someone, challenging those you cared about to do more and to do better than the status quo. The quote you so often communicated to me each time I left to go back to college was *"Do good."* Although it was simple in its essence, it was more dynamic from this perspective: Do the very best you can do, give 'em all you got and, at the very least, don't go out like a chump. Make them remember who and whose you are, so they never forget it. Leave an indelible impression on their minds. That way, whenever they see you coming, they already know you're going to bring it! That perspective is more intense and amplified.

You know the scripture says, *"For in Him [Christ] we live and move and have our being..."* (Acts 17:28).

The second part of that verse says, *"As even some of your own poets have said, for we too are his offspring."* The irony is, we are your offspring; together, you both have created spiritual Lions, and Dad fortified our upbringing as men of honor! (*Family of Lions*) I am reminded of the photo that hung in our living room on the wall. Symbolically, there was a family of lions, a pride. Just as it was five of us living among each other, the artwork depicted: Lion, lioness and the three young lions. We were raised to be lion-hearted in spirit. Many refer the lion to in essences being the king of their habitat, the jungle.

What did I do the day of graduation? I packed up my belongings, moved out of my apartment and headed back home to KC to start my new chapter of life as a post-graduate adult… another step in the human life cycle of maturity. It was the most exhilarating experience, to complete a life goal and to bless and honor my parents with an achievable accomplishment riddled with struggles and life lessons. May 1997, chapter closed: it was behind me.

Post-graduation, after moving back home to live with my parents (to save, plan and start a career and new chapter of life), there was much that needed to be done! But first, it was celebration time! As a graduation gift to me and my girlfriend (at that time), we took a vacation to Orlando… yes, Disney World! We planned this trip to embrace the start of what would become our new normal of life together while preparing for our wedding, scheduled for July 31, 1999.

We thoroughly enjoyed ourselves! Once we landed, we got our rental vehicle and drove to the hotel in Kissimmee Park. But the blessing is that during the drive, I stopped to get gas and ensure we were on the correct path to our hotel (that was life without Google Maps or Waze – it was June 1997, I was lucky to have a cell phone). Back in that era, you could pump the gas first and then pay afterwards, so after I topped off the gas tank, I went back in to pay. Inside the convenience store, a brother recognized my letters. We communicated from a distance, embraced and exchanged information. This was the biggest blessing I have experienced so far outside my normal comfort zone; it was almost too good to be true. Turns out, brotha graduated from Grambling State University (GSU) with an IT degree; at that time, he was in a leadership role for Disney World, which was exactly what we were there to visit. I reached out to him, and this brother and his girlfriend showed us around Orlando. We went out and ate together and finished the weekend visiting Daytona Beach. I never connected with that brotha again; I'd sure like to return the favor and treat him to a great time in my city: "The Home of Real BBQ," Kansas City (KC)!

Letter to Mom:

Mom, I'll share these experiences with you now because I never shared them with you while you were with us. I appreciate the life lessons you taught us throughout our development as your sons and young men. I think of you often, and I wonder: what would things be like with you still here? What would you think of my kids, your grandkids (the first grandkids in my generation you never met)? Would you be suffering from lupus and diabetes, plus living through the Covid pandemic with your underlying affliction? There are so many unknowns that would have concerned me about where we are as a country, a family and humanity as a whole. Most importantly, I would not have wanted you to be placed in any harmful situations or anything more that could potentially affect you negatively. But you left us too soon, I feel; you never met my kids, even though you wanted to meet them.

I can recall the time we were driving home on 72nd Street, by the old Dolgins and the waterslide. I remember the conversation like it was yesterday. You asked me if we were expecting. In my youthful and prompt response I replied, "No." Then, in a quiet, subtle voice, you merely said, "I just want to meet your kids one day." That day never came to fruition on earth, as we both know. I can only pray they meet you in the hereafter, in heaven. But know that I often struggle with that, as a father and as your son. Better yet, my heart aches because I could not see past my own youthful ambitions and immaturity at the time. Thus, the purpose of this book. I've always been your internal and curious child – well, that really hasn't changed a lot. I just try to channel my energy in other directions. It's probably easier to say that I deflect. In your case, I was deeply saddened; actually, broken, and still am. I did not realize it at the time, but I was depressed without a method of dealing with my grief and the loss of you. So, in deflective mode,

I wrote this letter, which is now a book. The idea was to express some of the things I had on my heart as it related to losing you. I did not just lose a mother. I lost a friend, a confidant, a wise woman, a teacher, as well as a mom. In its simplest form, a part of me died with you.

And perhaps I even wanted to, deep down inside. But God would not let it be so. So, again, in deflective mode (self-preservation), I told myself I needed a way to heal, to grieve and to channel my energy. I wanted to honor you all at the same time, which was a must! Yet, during my numbest days, I told myself, "If I can make it through this loss, I can make it through anything. Nothing else in life can hurt me this bad." Well, that's simply not true! Not only have I procrastinated with this project, I have become motivated and unmotivated, some days bewildered and perplexed as to why I'm even doing this. Why am I expressing myself in this way? What does this all mean? True to form, I have inadvertently pulled from the very thing I've tried so desperately not to rely on: my own faith.

See, you and Dad prayed, taught and fasted on our behalf… we were consecrated kids. Many people may not understand those very words, though some do. Mother, Cord B. Taylor put those values in y'all, and in turn, you put them in us. We have only been able to live life so long from your prayers and your lessons. At some point, it was imperative that I develop my own muscles of faith. I use the word "muscle" because, in its simplest form, our faith is but an interwoven group of tissues that (should) work together for greater efficiency towards a common goal, supported by tendons and ligaments that keep it all together for that goal. Simply put, I needed to exercise those muscles, grow and develop, provide protein and other nutrition to them to build and rebuild tissues that were broken or weakened by life's trials. Mom, that's hard! But you would always encourage us to try. Well, I'm trying. As much as it can hurt, I still need you as my encourager/confidant and supporter. You have always been my source of strength, encouragement and smiling reinforcement. You raised us all to believe we could do anything we put our minds to. I sure could use that type of support now, Mom. Unconditional and genuine regard without judgment, a calming nudge of support. You were our greatest cheerleader!

REFLECTION:

Mom, recall our first Thanksgiving as a married couple, Lorie and I. I was so excited to have you and dad over our new home for Thanksgiving dinner and I could not understand why my wife did not have that same measure of excitement. Although Lorie and I had work through that moments as a newly married couple, we pushed through it. Lorie and I made the best meal we could have made together for you and dad. As your son I felt honored to be able to give back to you both, as my parents something you gave to me all my life…Love, togetherness and what I thought was a good meal. What you never did was made me feel as your son I had to choose between my wife or you, I was so blessed not to have a self mom, but instead a wise mom.

Many moms do not understand that fundamental mother-son dynamic and many mothers blindly still only see their baby-boy. Not the grown man they have raised, the husband, man and father in many cases that must now be a leader for his family. Conversely, many new wives do not carefully know how to make a smooth transition from girlfriend to wife without making her husband fell he has to choose. All these things smooth out over time and much conversation! Which, we endured; although I felt some kind of way, we still broke bread together. It took years for me to divulge that aspect of the conversation with Lorie.

That was the first and last Thanksgiving we had with you, you pasted months later in March. Thank you for coming, spending the night and dining with us in our new home. It was an honor for us to have hosted you and dad. Thank you for understanding the moment.

My wife, Lorie – Mom, I know you can recall all those visits we shared whenever I came home (which was generally every other week). I know at times it felt like she was pulling me away from you. And I know that troubled your heart, in a motherly way. You and I talked about this before, though; recall the moment we talked on the edge of the bed after our first major break-up? Well, keeping in step with that conversation, she has been a blessing in my life in so many aspects! Mom, she mothered and continues to mother our children – she's my girl! And I want you to understand, she has given me peace, love and our children… I'll forever be grateful to her for choosing to sacrifice herself physically and psychologically in the birthing of our children. And, Mom, before we had kids and built a home together, we actually constructed our present home, which is different from our marriage home, the only home of ours you were able to see. But I know you have been watching us from the heavens, and I'm not just saying that. We are all at Godly peace knowing you earned your wings here on earth while you were here, and that cannot be argued!

Recall the last job I applied for – we "touched and agreed on it," right? It was USPS. Well, I actually got that job, Mom. But weeks later, I received a call from an auto manufacturing company. It paid more, so I resigned from USPS, even though we prayed and "touched and agreed on it." Against my better judgment, I worked there as a FLS (Frontline Supervisor) for 3.5 years. Then 9/11 hit and the market took a downward turn, and they downsized my line and outsourced the parts we were producing on-site. Well, I lost my position as a byproduct of those economic downturns. At the age of 26, your son was actively building a new home and had a career job making +$90,000 annually up until this economic downturn.

Well, my wife was there for me, Mom. She didn't emasculate me as a man and as the man of the household. Instead, she embraced me. Mom, I can recall the drive home trying to think to myself, how does a man tell his wife (a black woman), "Honey, I lost my career job and I'm headed home"? I actually wanted to leave, but I did not have a real destination to drive to. She embraced me, she did not look down on me as a man, and instead she encouraged me. Mom, that's why I selected her; I didn't know how she could take all that, but she took it with grace as I witnessed you do with dad! What that did for me, as a man was nothing short of inspirational! You already know that as your son, I elevated my game all the more! I worked harder to regain employment, and once we did, it was a definite lower salary, but I had no real choice but to make the best of it and I did!

Once Lorie delivered your grandkids, she solidified and cemented her partnership with me as my wife. Mom, you would love your grandkids. Evin is now 15 years old. He has his learner's permit to drive. He likes girls, but somehow has an unwavering determination to become an electrical engineer (EE). That drives him more than pursuing girls now. He loves soccer, and he wants nothing more than to go to college for EE and play soccer. He has an aspiration of playing soccer on an Olympic and European level. Aren't those lofty goals? Not really. I have full faith and confidence in him too! He will be all he desires to be, and then some!

He's a kind young man, strong and handsome. He's on the honor roll; he seldom makes anything less than a B. He's preparing for ACTs now as a sophomore. He's culturally aware and participates in Black Student Union (BSU) in high school. Remember, I was in that while in college, but imagine this, Mom – he's doing this for himself, as an awareness of his life, his heritage and his own curiosities. He's never caused us an ounce of trouble. Well, his elementary days were challenging for us, especially me, as he has some of the same characteristics I had as a young boy. But I digress.

Mom, your granddaughter is a pearl; I recall that being the prettiest piece of jewelry you owned. She has brown skin, a rich, caramel, smooth skin tone. She is witty! Confident. She wants to be a famous actor. She thinks she's so smart and everyone else is not as smart as she is. She's going through a phase now; she thinks she is right about everything! Her whole goal in life is to contradict me and prove me wrong. Mom, is that an innate girl thing? I guess I'll truly never know, because you're not here to help guide me through this season of my life. I'm reminded of the old church song we'd hear the old folks singing sometimes, "Somebody Prayed for Me." Oddly enough, your grandson and I prayed for her: he wanted a sister and I wanted a daughter. Thank God, He listened and heard our prayers, and blessed us with her. But, boy… we didn't know what we were praying for, huh! She'll do great things, Mom. Both of them will!

My prayer: Please continue to watch over us! Guide our hearts and spirits, and enlighten the pathway for His purpose. Mom, I ask that you please keep a hedge of protection around Dad. He needs you so bad! You all had a special thing going on. Cover and protect all your grandkids and my brothers and sisters. I say a special prayer for Aunt Wendy; she and Tracy miss you immensely. I know your siblings miss you dearly. Well, I guess I can't ask for much more without wishing you back here. Looks like I have to go. I love you and will never forget you. As I close, with a full spirit and tears of sadness and loss, I press on… trying to *"do good."*

Just last night, February 6, I had the opportunity to talk with my dad, who by the grace of God is still in his right mind and has a reasonable portion of health at 75 years, young. In reflection, he told me why we, the Baileys, have a commitment to responsible work expectations as men in the Bailey family. Only he can be so detailed in sharing his experiences being raised by his grandpa. Papa's full name was Leonard Milton Bailey; he was born on July 10, 1887, and he was from Oklahoma. There was only him and another brother, Benjamin Bailey (who moved to Louisiana), and their parents' names were Edward and Mary Bailey. Great-grandpa was a teacher for many years in the White Church community. However, he had a strong sense of being an outdoorsman over classroom stability. He became a farmer for over 50 years, farming mostly berries and vegetables on 20 acres. (Our family later lost this property due to repayment of gambling debts.) On the weekends, he'd take his fruits and vegetables to the 38th and State Avenue corner market area to sell his produce. Keep in mind, he rode a horse-drawn carriage from near 91st Street on the outskirts of the White Church community to 38th and State Avenue – that's 7.8 miles in each direction.

He then married my great-grandmother, Eva Monroe. She too was greatly known in her community as a baker, and she leveraged her baking talents throughout the Quindaro community. She taught her Bailey daughters, Cecilia, Marion, Grace and Gertrude, how to prepare original piecrust and create the berry pie filling. My Auntie Cecilia made the best apple pie in the world! But I digress. My great-grandmother's sons were Adrian Bailey, Leonard Bailey, Jr., and another son who died at the age of nine. She passed away in 1935; I'm not sure of the cause, but she was greatly missed by her family and community. She was a wise woman, in her time; on her deathbed, she asked her best friend to marry her husband because she was familiar with her family and kids. Later, Great-grandpa Leonard did marry Myrtle Robinson; she later passed in 1956. He passed in 1962 at KU at 6:05 pm from an illness.

It was for the funeral service of Great-grandpa Leonard Bailey that my dad, Pastor Charles "Chuck" Bailey, Sr., was told to stay at home and not to attend by his mother, Marion (Bailey) Oliver. My father ran away that evening to stay with Uncle Adrian and Edith Coggs. The more I dig into to historical family facts, the more I learn. Again, I digress. The main point of this is the innate Bailey work ethic that was and still is being fostered as we unconsciously and consciously pass those same values to the generations to come.

As you can see and understand, "out of struggle great people are forged" – it's out of the circumstances of struggle that they are made! My point in sharing this brief history from my father's side of the family was to give reference and pay deference to his making, the way he fashioned and groomed me from his experiences. The Bailey commitment to family, marriage and the raising of one's family is a hardwired core value that our family finds solace in. I know this because I have modeled our life with those same values: to provide, protect and give guidance unto my seeds and hopefully the next generation after my kids. I love you both, Evin and Alana, and I pray that in some form, I'm able to leave a positive legacy for you both, as your great-great-grandfather attempted to do for our family. Know that you have the propensity to love, be committed and cherish family. It was infused into you both, genetically; it's a part of your DNA. Know that however responsible and committed to it you choose to be, you have a genetic code and consecrated prayers that bind these all together.

Therefore, choose your partners and spouses with this in mind! Remember to support and uphold Great-grandfather's core values, regardless of superficial substance/presentation or vain words. They must love God, as He loved the church and gave his life for that cause. There will be many who look the part, but recall our conversations, lessons and acts you witnessed throughout your development and life. And know that "no one person is an island" by themselves; everyone has someone in their life who has helped them. Helping someone won't dim your God-given light, but it will instead enhance your talents, gifts and abilities. Your plight has been divinely ordered for you to become great purposeful parents, whenever the Lord sees fit for you. You'll know when – it will reveal itself.

When Lorie and I got married on July 31, 1999, we were blessed to go from a home to a "home together." Let me explain. We met early in the eighth grade, lived in the same neighborhood, and attended Arrowhead Middle School together (in fact, we rode the same bus up through high school). We knew of each other through a mutual friend, Ms. Andrea Macklin (a family-church friend), but she didn't care for me, and I didn't much care for her either. By senior year, I was a strong student-athletic multi-sport letterman, playing varsity football and wrestling (let's just say track did not end well for me – long story).

I recall a mutual classmate told me, "She likes you and talks about you often in class and whenever you are walking throughout the hallways during school." I was a member of the school journalism photography team, so I had hall passes to access and get classmates out of class (read between the lines). Well, one day, I decided to look into it. Her history teacher was the varsity basketball coach, Chuck Minor, who everyone loved. So, I stopped by the classroom and asked her to come out into the hallway for interviewing purposes, and she did. We walked and talked; within 20-30 minutes, I returned her to class, but I believe we exchanged phone numbers. (She no longer lived in my neighborhood, as her family had moved by that time.)

Well, this was our senior year. We continued to talk: days became weeks, weeks became months, etc. During our courtship, we were approaching the end of our high school journey; prom was just around the corner. Because all was still good with us, we decided to go to prom together. It was great, we had fun! We kept progressing at the boyfriend and girlfriend level. Shortly thereafter, though, it was time to graduate, and at the same time, I was being recruited and going on college recruiting trips as much as possible, mostly on weekends. During graduation, things got weird between us – it's like we were getting bored with each other. So, our relationship slowed down. That was okay with me, because the recruiting trips kept it interesting, to say the least! Plus, my aunt and cousin were going to drive up from Muskogee, OK, to attend my graduation, so, I really had to belt down and complete the remaining math objectives (5 of 30) I still needed to complete before I would be eligible for graduation. I completed my last five objectives and graduated, "thank-the-lardy," from F.L. Schlagle, class of '91.

Oddly, our relationship was never a complete break-up, but more of a pause. During the summer, we reconnected and came to the conclusion that we were not done with each other yet. So, although I would go on to play football out of town, we continued to call and write, and on occasion, she'd ride down with my parents for family day and homecoming games. After a year and half away, I graduated with my Associate of Arts degree. Because my GPA was well over 3.0 as a student-athlete, I had options. Upon returning to KCK, I got a job as a paraprofessional teacher, where I fell in love with being in the classroom and influencing kids, just like I did as the juniors' Sunday school teacher at church.

I applied for an academic scholarship to become an educator. Because of my above-average GPA, I qualified. After obtaining that academic scholarship, I set off to go back to college, and during that time, Lorie and I became engaged. I thought I could be engaged and away at school simultaneously. Nah, that didn't work well. After a failed attempt at being engaged, we returned to boyfriend and girlfriend status… this was a challenging time for us! My position was that without finishing the goals we set out to attain, we were selling ourselves short, and I've never been a fan of not completing my task and goals; plus, I wanted the same for her too!

Holding fast to my convictions, I was accepted and enrolled into the University of Arkansas at Pine Bluff to complete an undergraduate degree in teaching. However, as I already described, Mom asked me to go to a closer school. My girlfriend was also not happy about UAPB, even though her dad's side of the family was from that same community, and she communicated her displeasure. Because of the influences of both ladies in my life,

I acquiesced and attended ESU. We continued our love affairs as boyfriend and girlfriend; however, it wasn't long before she broke up with me. (Summer of 1997 – I'll get into it later.) We got back together at the end of that summer, and since we had both graduated with our undergrad degrees, we celebrated by going to Disney World Resort in Kissimmee, FL.

However, between 1997 and 1999, I stayed with my parents and worked on career plans. This is key: I was the only one living with my parents at that time, as all my siblings were out of the house. During that time, I had an amazing opportunity to witness the greatest example of marriage, love and commitment. I witnessed my father and mother exemplify the values of marriage in 3D. Although I stayed in the basement, modestly helping out around the house (cutting grass, paying for groceries on occasion, but mostly paying off student loans and rebuilding my creditworthiness), I learned from my seasoned parents what marriage and long-term (longsuffering) commitment meant. This example has served to be invaluable in our current 23 years of holy matrimony.

Once my wife had our kids, especially the last one, our daughter, I knew she was "my girl." Why do I say that? Because it was at that point I knew she was all in, as was I. Plus, by that time, I knew, by Mom and Dad's precept and example, what marriage was supposed to look like: love each other, honor our values and make each other better versions of ourselves. So, recall that a boyfriend and girlfriend relationship is what we started out with; now, it has blossomed from having been young, committed-but-unseasoned lovers to developing into a partnership of bonding and commitment. Don't get me wrong, we've had more than a few quagmires throughout the years, but we have always, by the grace of God, been able to stay committed and connected to one another and build our home together – metaphorically, brick by brick. See, it's not the bricks that are the most important parts of the relationships; it's the clay, the cement that fortifies the marriage bond. That's the bonding agent that fortifies the relationship from both foreign and domestic attacks. It literally keeps the elements outside of itself. That applies to both internal and external factors in all facets of the lifecycle of marriage.

Letter to Mom:

Mom, the grandson you never met was very clever as a baby! Technology has evolved more than you could imagine from the '90s. (Remember how elated you were to have an email account and desktop computer in my old room? I digress.) As new parents, we wanted to keep our intimacy on fire, yet still be able to see or monitor your grandson. So, we purchased a digital camera, with live audio and heartbeat-monitoring pad – I'm sure you'd be looking at me with the side-eye if you were here. This baby monitoring system allows us to view and listen in on them as they actively breathe, play and sleep.

As he developed and grew, we noticed from time to time that he'd find a way out of his bed. Lorie would ask me if I had let him out of his bed to play in his room, and I'd reply "no" and then ask why. She'd say, "Well, he out his crib playing." This happened increasingly often, and vice-versa. It happened so often that we started questioning one another and our ability to be honest with each other.

Well, one day, we both just watched him together. Boy, was that a treat! We discovered that he was climbing out of his bed by himself. We were aghast! We were treating one another ill and starting to second-guess each other, which wasn't good. Because this was our first kid, neither of us wanted to be "that person" (the one who failed or didn't grow and develop our son the right way). But that just highlights the mothering (grand-mothering) you are missing out on and do not get to experience as you did before with all your other grandkids. It's not that you are not experiencing them, because I know you are looking down on us as our heavenly angel. It's just different for me not seeing you experience this journey with us, although you're in your heavenly place.

Know that he's a clever guy! On the honor roll, 3.7 GPA, thus far with advanced classes – Advanced Geometry, Algebra 2, Robotics – and he's a big history lover. As an added certification, he is signed up to take classes at the local technical school to pick up additional understanding of Aerospace and Electronics coursework. He plans to play soccer for the USA in the Olympics and earn an Electrical Engineering (EE) degree. He's an amazing son, spirit and joy to be around; I know you'd fall in love with him. He helps out at church with the sound and video ministry, working the sound booth (around electronics, imagine that). He loves to read! He recently turned 16, April 4th 2022; he already has his driver's permit. Mom, I find myself yelling at him because driving a vehicle is a serious and responsible engagement for average folks each day. But your son is interested in driving a stick-shift manual car. Funnily enough, I have a 6-speed turbo-charged Mini Cooper – you would have loved it! It reminds me of the powder-blue Super Beetle you had. We've been out working on it, – I'm getting better, less yelling and more of a calm, assertive tone, which seems to be working better than the yelling. But Dad yelled at us…I suppose times have changed and are still changing!

Alana, as well, is our heartbeat! Mom, she's a beautiful brown-skinned little lady with densely thick and long curly hair. She is currently nine, going on 25! She loves to travel already! We've taken the kids to Frederick, MD, Miami, FL, Pine Bluff, AR, Texas, Costa Rica and the Disney Cruise. I just might have set her expectations too high for the young man of her future (whoever that is). I'm teaching her your craft, and she enjoys baking things! At first, she did not like the lemon cake, but guess what, I'm teaching her how to bake it, and she loves it! She is mentally sharp, spicy in spirit and thinks she is the household comedian. She loves dancing and gymnastics too! A few years back, she won several medals in a gymnastics tournament at Xtreme Gymnasium. At church, she is engaged in Interpretative Dance ministry.

Interesting enough, dating back several generations, from Dad's grandmother (Great-grandma Eva) to Mom's Aunt Minnie, baking and southern cuisine has always been in our family heritage. As kids, we'd always have family reunions on the Thomas side of the family (Mom's), and you'd always have the older men of the family there churning ice cream for the kids, and the seasoned women of the family managing the food and attempting to keep the kids/men of the family out of the food until after grace was given).

The food was so diverse! Greens, cabbage, baked beans (with chunks of bacon), fried corn, BBQ chicken/ribs/brisket/sausage, and every cookout has to have hot dogs and hamburgers. For dessert, we would have a plethora of pies, cakes, cupcakes, cobblers and any other pastry you could imagine from an African-American home. All my cousins would find us and ask, "So, where is your mom's food?" It did not matter if it was her potato salad, baked beans, greens or cakes/cobblers. They would find and select only the dishes she prepared and try to get her cakes before Aunt Wheelie would see them, because she patrolled the tables and would run you off with a flyswatter. As kids, we perceived her as being mean, but in actuality, she was merely trying to be sanitary, orderly and family-oriented. In other words, it's literally nasty to put your finger or personal utensil in an open buffet-style dish that everyone has to eat from before saying grace over it and using a serving utensil.

Furthermore, we would eat in the following order: men (though oftentimes they would defer to the kids), children, teenagers and then the women would typically eat last. The only sense I saw in that was that, back then, every man was the provider. The point was to get every family there so everyone could learn and get to know their relatives – well, you know why, right? Oddly enough, several of the men on my mom's side of the family worked at Wilson's packinghouse, in an old area of the Armourdale community of Kansas City, KS, and at last check, they still have an annual or biannual Armourdale community reunion. Again, the point I gleaned from this was about family; it has always been about family from my perspective.

Bringing this back home to our family, many may recall the time in the life of the Bailey household when Mom was diagnosed with lupus and later diabetes. This was in the mid-'80s. Both Mom and Dad brought us together for a family meeting, and it was at that time that we learned of this affliction being placed on my mom's shoulders (which were essentially our shoulders too, as a family unit). We had a mixture of both pessimism and optimism. Why? Because we were a faithful and praying family! Pessimism because of the uncertainty of what lupus was back then and the ramifications it could have, yet optimism because we had her back in every sense of the phrase and believed we would all do our best to see her through those times. (As I type this, I cry because of those moments.)

I recall that during that family meeting, she and Dad showed us her back. Not understanding how this was all relevant at the time, we were shown two or three flat lesions (patches) in the upper-mid area of her back (near the major/minor rhomboid area). The depth of the scarring of her skin was at least to the dermis layer. How could a kid know this? Because I recall my father cleaning and dressing her back. Many times, as onlookers, my brothers and I watched my dad carefully wipe down the scabs of these lesion-like patches from her back, often with fluids oozing or seeping out of her skin. The passion a boy has for his mother runs deep! As we watched, we paid attention to her facial expressions and his hands, making sure our dad did not hurt her or cause her to be in any discomfort, and we would often retrieve cotton balls to keep everything sanitary and clean. To that point, was that lupus? We were kids; we did not really know. All we did know was that we were going to rally around her in whatever the circumstances were, to care for the queen of our home. My apologies if this seems graphic to some, but I need you to understand my feelings as a young man during this time of family care and togetherness.

By the end of these types of moments as a family unit, we would have purpose in our daily lives. My dad took an offer to become a supervisor at his job; they had asked him several times before my mom's bout with her afflictions. For that matter, we all stepped up to cover her and cover for her – two different effects. My oldest brother got a career job with the UAW. I continued my education, played both football and wrestling and held down a job to cover my personal expenses and avoid putting anything on my parents or siblings. I worked at the local Ace Hardware store and Taco Bell, along with any job I could do to offset expenses and lessen the burden of our household budget on my dad.

What this did was open the door for Mom to stop working, although she hated the notion of not making her own money or being able to contribute to the economics and edification of her household. She took great pride in being a builder of her home, men (father and kids) and her siblings; she felt it was her task to be an advisor and counselor to all of us. But, with this extra time on her hands, she decided to take a few classes. She enrolled in the local technical school, which was known as AVTS (Area Vocational Technical School) back then. She took decorative cake-baking classes and later earned her certificate in that program. See, mom was a finisher! All throughout my upbringing, she preached, "Finish what you start, and if someone else brings something to you, you finish that too." That resonated within me educationally, task-wise and just commitment-wise. She was exemplifying that in her daily walk while dealing with a new and unknown disease, lupus. Later, we understood that this was a black women's disease.

She used those same skills to make the impacts she could. She was known for her lemon cake, which she taught me how to bake as well. But those classes taught her more than just how to perfect her desserts (especially cakes)! Those classes taught her patience, that everything under the sun (Son, whom she worshipped) had a process to go through. They taught that with the proper ingredients and a special touch of love, God can manifest something beautiful out of any situation, if only you sincerely believe (Hebrews 11:6) with the faith of a child (Matthew 18), knowing that God can and will deliver you out with grace, tender loving care and kindness.

Mom later showcased her skills and started making wedding cakes. My dad, brother and I would drive all around the city setting up her wedding cakes. We made sure there were no cracks in the icing for her customers and, most of all, their wedding cakes were as tasteful as their memories of perfection were in those moments. She was intentional. She wanted the best for people, not being envious of others but making the best of her sphere. Touching those around her in the best way she could or know how too. Earlier in the book, I mentioned continuing this tradition of baking her infamous lemon cake. I can make several other types of her cakes, but this particular cake was one that everyone loved! Was it the tart taste? The sugary sweetness? Or the amount of love she put into it?

Many times, I heard her say to her sisters on the phone that she "put her foot in it." In layman's terms, she showed out, meaning she did impressive, sincere work and/or did her best to make a memorable and impactful moment. It was in those moments that we would talk, just her and me, about everything – the desires of her heart and mine. These were intimate moments with my mom, outside of me taking her on the occasional mother/son dates. You see, my oldest brother was raising his own family and managing his own household, while my younger brother was in college in Pittsburg, KS. My older sister was raising my niece and nephew, again in her own household as well (which I got the pleasure of being fully engaged in as an uncle). My point is, it was just Mom, Dad and me for years. I got the privilege of seeing what a mature marriage looks like, which was valuable to my life and a huge blessing.

During some of these kitchen moments, my dad thought he needed to come into the kitchen to give his cooking advice, and boy did I antagonize hostility and confusion between them too, trying to provoke an argument or disagreement, but it was all in fun! Besides, it never worked. In moments of true competition in the kitchen, Mom would taste Dad's dish, and after he left the kitchen, she would calmly throw a dash or pinch of salt/pepper or seasoning into his dish, unbeknownst to him. I would snigger in laughter, because he had no clue Mom was actually, in a discreet way, making his dish more appealing and appetizing to the palate. I digress. My main point was that, during our kitchen time, she would pass on wise words: "Kevin, not everyone is going to like you," "do things to the best of your ability" and *"Finish what you start."*

My mom was very wise. Looking back now, she prepared us for everything and everybody, those near and far. Read between those lines yourself.

There was a moment in my life where as a guy, I would have failed significantly. My mom found out I was in love with a young lady and that the young lady had dumped me. Lorie. I was a total wreck internally and externally. I was literally lovesick. I had been crying, didn't have any appetite and was still throwing up. In between those moments, I would continue to read this letter basically begging on paper for her to take me back. This was a defining moment in my quest to woo the opposite sex as a young man. And Mom knew I was failing horribly, even as her son! As you've read, we loved hard. Hard things fall quickly! After my fall, she was there as a mom, as my confidant. She sat me down on the edge of the bed, and I read the letter to her with tears in my eyes, from a broken heart. She asked me two questions:

1) What were her last words to you?

2) Can you live life without her?

After answering both questions, I continued to explain to her that if I could just go to her house and give her this letter I wrote, she would take me back… and in true mom mode, she said "no." She said, "Give her what she asked for: space. Leave her alone." Later that evening, I saw my ex-girlfriend at the local QT where we were fueling our cars. We spoke, but then she looked at me and saw that I was not looking well. In fact, she asked me, "Are you okay?" I can't remember how I responded at the time, but the fact of the matter was, I was still extremely lovesick over her. In that moment, my mom taught me to go on about my business; to seek out the desires of my heart, minus her. So, I did, and it was not easy. Her point was that you couldn't impose yourself on someone (a young lady) who does not like you anymore. (Recall our kitchen conversations.) The power of that insight was pivotal in my ability to move on, survive lost love and have a healthy relationship with the opposite sex while maintaining my dignity as a young, brokenhearted male.

Months later, my best friend was at the last party of the summer, and my ex-girlfriend ran into him. Wouldn't you know it, she asked about me? She later called to check in on me. I was over it by then, so I immediately answered the phone with confidence and certainty: "What is it? What do you want? Why are you calling me now?" As you can see, I had fully recovered and was no longer lovesick, but instead galvanized and resolute in my manhood. But we later talked, and those talks became college visits. I resumed life with the understanding of what love, being lovesick and healing truly meant. Obviously, we later progressed from dating, to engagement and then marriage. Thank you, Mom, for that profound life lesson for that season or moment in the life of a lovesick son.

After Mom passed, as you would know, we inevitably had to go through her cherishable earthly possessions to sort out. We collected and sorted through photos, and her dresses were given to her sisters. But the most precious item of hers was almost overlooked: her plants. You see because my mom was a green-thumb nurturer, we all heard early on from childhood how to care for her plants. Now it was time to put those listening moments into practice. I'm not sure how this happened, but I somehow took home the mother-in-law's-tongue, which we've had since we were kids. Once I took possession of this plant, all her teachings kicked in. I started with distilled water until I could get fresh rainwater. Once I was able to collect several water jugs, it was all good! I re-educated myself by reading up on that particular plant's needs and cross-referenced information with my aunts (her sisters). It was on and poppin from there.

Mom passed on March 19, 2000, at the age of 55. It's 2022, and the mother plant is still thriving! Actually, within that time, that same plant has been split at least four or five times. Each brother has a plant, and I believe two nieces have them as well, if I recall correctly. You see, it's not that I'm the best green-thumb guy, but just know that I listened to my mom – she was worth listening to. After making the split, I replaced the soil with jet-black fresh soil. The value in that was huge! The plant grew so fast that I had to start a new pot; I now have two five-gallon pots in my home alone. The plant is thriving!

Follow this metaphor: in life, there are times when we need new, nutritionally enriched soil to germinate in. The fresh soil has additives, oxygenated dirt packed with rejuvenated properties that yield nothing but positive outcomes. Now combine that with fresh rainwater from the heavens and just the right amount of sun/Son, and new growth and development is inevitable. The process of photosynthesis is the guaranteed outcome.

In the end, the plants are still thriving! I believe the refreshed dirt was pivotal in the next level of growth for these plants. Even in rich soil, conditions are such that anything can realistically grow and thrive, but the soil helps sustain the life of the plant, providing much-needed nutritional values and properties that foster beneficial life and longevity.

The correlation here is in the humanity of my willingness to listen, which worketh patience (James 1:2-4)! I merely slowed down enough to listen to my mother, and I watched her demonstration in action. Words only go so far. The greater lesson is experiencing the demonstration of how it all comes together. Mom taught us with wisdom beyond her years; the blessing is that she was my mom, and I paid attention to all her lessons.

As I wake up this morning refreshed and charged to do the will of my Heavenly Father, which art in heaven, I thank God for the breath of life, reason, portions of health (given my ethnicity, genetic factors and choices) and my family. As I wrap up this journey of Life After Her, "her" being Evelyn "Teenie" (Thomas) Bailey, let me provide some context to the poem you'll read at the end of this book.

I must reflect on my friendships. I have always had a small circle of male brothers. I can call them brothers because we have lived together, I know their families, their families know my family and they know we are as thick as… well, I digress. I call them my brothers! It's not that I don't already have two outstanding biological brothers, Charles "Chuck" Bailey, Jr., and Durail Allen Bailey, because I do! The point of this is to explain this other brotherhood. You see, I have been told that when God gives you something, it's intended for you. These two brothers were in fact given to me by God Himself. I wasn't looking for them; we found each other: House & K-Gee.

House has a family connection. His family, the Buie's, lived on Garfield Street with my mom's family. As you know, back in those days, neighbors shared sugar, flour and other materials until payday or until they could get to the store to purchase their own supply. Oddly enough, I didn't meet House until we were teenagers. We worked together at Taco Bell. Even stranger, my now-wife and my best friend K-Gee also worked with me at Taco Bell – we all worked together and attended the same high school, F.L. Schlagle, under the leadership of Principal Carl Bruce (member of Kappa Alpha Psi, Fraternity Inc.).

K-Gee and I met in the eighth grade, and we have been best friends all our lives. We met this strange dude named Scott Allen Buie, a.k.a. House, who had transferred from Kalamazoo, MI, to Kansas City, KS. He was a year ahead of both K-Gee and me, and a lot more mature than us, given his upbringing, era in time, family dynamics and the city he came from. He was game-tight, from the streets – he was streetwise, wearing FUBU and Karl Kani gear. He was a stout, athletic young man, and so was I.

We were on the wrestling team and football team together. I introduced, taught and sparred with him, and this dude took that training all the way to the KS State wrestling finals in the 189 weight class, placing second in his first season of wrestling ever. Man, the first few weeks of wrestling, I was putting it on him – you know, letting him have it! As brothers, we were competitive! By the third week, he developed that dawg mentality too.

At Taco Bell, I was a cooker, working in the back. I noticed him walking by, heading to count his drawer or register drawer; he dropped a $20 bill on the floor and kept walking. I was the only one that noticed it at the time. At this point, I had a few options: swiftly walk over to the dropped $20 bill and pick it up for myself (we had no cameras in that blind spot), or let him know he dropped it and save him from getting fired for a short drawer count. I choose the latter. He thanked me, and we became best friends for life after that! So much so, he lived with us at 539 South 73rd Street for a period of time. We shared stories about girls we desired to date, etc. and formed an unbreakable bond, as now he was a member of the Bailey household. We shared clothes (trendy clothing, which we called "gear"), food and room. We played on the same college football team together. Because he was a year older than me, I kind of watched him go off to play at Butler County Community College (BCCC), and then the following year, we both attended BCCC.

The whole point of this is to share this background and history so you understand why he was on the program at Mom's funeral and why he wrote the poem at the end of this book. Again, this speaks to the impact of the Bailey household that Teenie cultivated. It's because he lived it! He lived in the Bailey household, so that makes him family and gives credence to his poem and telling of what he witnessed, in rhythmic fashion, while in our home as my "Brother from another Mother," as we like to say. To him, Evelyn "Teenie" Bailey was the Queen Bee!

FINAL

This is it...

Poem for Mrs. Bailey:

Mostly known by her cakes and pies, so appropriate for a woman with so much sweetness and spiritually filled inside. A peaceful smile just to let you know, your time is always worth her while, always willing to give a helping hand just to let you know you're not alone, and if no one else feels you, Mrs. Bailey understands.

Always longing to share her hand in prayer, just to let you know no matter what battles you are going through, you're still in God's hands. A shoulder to cry on and a hand to hold, always giving warmth when the world treats you cold. She'll open her doors to share with all, holding nothing back, implying it's never too late to make a comeback.

Her home she keeps holy, also a place for rest, a sanctuary from God to help ease life's test, and for that fact alone, I know Mrs. Bailey's home will always remain blessed. Her home was first and never neglected, young wives can learn if they see from Mrs. Bailey's perspective. Her husband she treated just like a king, he was her honey and she his Queen B. The reason why I say this is 'cause I seen it. Her home was full of love and always kept neat, and if you ever came over, she was one of those old-school moms that always offered you something to eat.

She was loved by her patients and would lift you in her prayers, a God-fearing woman, and to the young people who knew her, she was far from square. She would tell us the truth and wouldn't fall for our lies. We might have thought we was getting away, but Mrs. Bailey had a way of letting us know we just got by.

The legacy she left will be passed down, for what she was given was from her spirit, soul and God-centered mind. We hate to see you go, but we couldn't hold you back. Your spirit is set free, and you're right where God would have you be. Mrs. Bailey ran a good race and fought a good fight with the only weapon she had truth about, Christ and a godly lifestyle that proves it's right. You see, Mrs. Bailey stayed up, prayed up, preached up and stored up her riches in Heaven, which she did in sincerity; now she's gone to collect her prize and will enjoy it for eternity.

Scott Allen Buie

Letter to Mom:

In short, you were my first experience of loving and understanding the opposite gender. You were my number one cheerleader, even when I didn't know how valuable that was or what it would mean for me moving forward in life as a male. You were my confidant. You taught practical considerations for dealing with this thing we call humanity; you showed me the difference between empathy and sympathy. You taught me to do good, and you instilled in me confidence, determination and completion of an assignment.

Don't quit! The breaking of day is upon you, if you are steadfast, and He will smile upon you. God honors those who are obeisant to His will. You taught me what discretion should look like from a woman's perspective and what women notice about a man. You drilled love into my head. You were wise! Thank you for that baking time, even though we both know it wasn't about baking… it was about our personal connection in those moments, mother to son.

Many times, I feel and believe that we are all coasting through life off the backs of your prayers, moments of consecrated prayers and those closet prayers you used to pray for us. I still recall your favorite scripture: Psalm 91, "Qui habitat" in Latin, which means "who lived." You still live in our hearts and minds, and your spirit continues in the lives of your grandkids, siblings, friends. You know that every year (on Mother's Day and August 1), we are reminded of March 19, 2000, when God, in His infinite wisdom, led you to your eternal resting place in Heaven. We know you do not have to prick yourself to check your blood sugar levels anymore, your lesions of lupus on your back don't bleed anymore and you don't need your feet rubbed anymore.

As much as you are no longer present on the earth, your spirit in its angelic form hovers over each of us in an omnipresent aura. I realize God has you busy and on assignment for His eternal will of the Kingdom, but my earthly spirit yearns for your conversation and guidance (Isaiah 26:9). Sometimes, I dream about you, only to have to wake up and not see you. Continue to talk to me in my dreams. You have inspired us all to "*do good.*" Please keep us in your prayers; we all pray that if it's in His will, we shall see you again. I personally pray that this act of honoring you is evidence I will *never* forget how you impacted our lives. Hugs and kisses, and continue to rest in heaven, Evelyn "Teenie" Bailey.

LIFE, AFTER HER!

My sister Evelyn Thomas-Bailey (Teenie) meant so much to me. She took care of me like one of her own kids, especially since I was her baby sister/daughter, and for that I will always be thankful. We shared a love for shopping early on. It would be just about every Monday morning, after we had our big breakfast at our mom Lillie Thomas's house, and everyone who knew our mother knew she could COOK. After breakfast, we would strike out on our shopping ventures buying clothes, shoes, jewelry, etc, always looking for and finding the best deals. Teenie would always pick out the best outfits for everyone, making sure everything matched to a T.

My sister was hands down one of the best dressed of all time! I knew and learned so much from her style and elegance. She will always be well respected for helping family, friends, and others during her ministries. Whenever anyone needed help, it didn't matter if it was a hot meal, clothing, or a place to stay, she would always be willing to help. That's why she's missed so much by her family and friends, but will live in my heart and the hearts of all her loved ones forever!

Love you,
your baby sister,
Nina Thomas-Black (Nini)

LIFE, AFTER HER!

When I think about my sister Evelyn Thomas-Bailey, I recall her nickname "Teenie." There's a lot of beautiful moments and memories we shared as siblings, and that can last a lifetime. She was a legacy in my heart, as well as other siblings too. Growing up with two older sisters, Bessie Thomas-Canady and Evelyn Thomas-Bailey, they were our sibling caretakers, as well as caring for their other younger siblings. My two older sisters cooked for us when our mom Lillie Thomas was tired, especially for Sunday dinners!

Teenie always made sure we had dessert with our meals. Both of my sisters had best friends who would come over to eat on Sundays with our family, but we had to wait until they arrived and ate first before we could break bread. Back in those days, company ate first, out of courtesy (this era is gone).

As sisters, we shared a room together, and Teenie *always* made sure I kept the room in the same condition she did. I was a flower girl in her wedding, and she also helped me get hired at Kansas University Medical Center, where she was employed. Teenie was such a philanthropist in spirit, even before the term was a thing.

But most of all, Evelyn Thomas-Bailey to me (and to all her other siblings) was a strong and **GOD-FEARING** sister, mother, and devoted wife. We loved her very dearly.

Forever Love, Sis!

Rosemary

www.ingramcontent.com/pod-product-compliance
Lightning Source LLC
Chambersburg PA
CBHW062115080426
42734CB00012B/2880